The Family of Jesus

Timeless Lessons for Modern Families

Gerald Vaughn "Jerry" Drummonds II

DEDICATION

To my beloved wife KD,

Your unwavering love and support are the foundation of our family. This book is a testament to the strength, joy, and wisdom you've brought into our lives. Thank you for being my partner in this beautiful journey of family. Everything I am and all that I create is made richer because of you.

With all my love,

Jerry

Copyright © May 15, 2018, 2024
Registration Number – TXu 2-098-322
From Benchmark Living
by Gerald Vaughn "Jerry" Drummonds II

All rights reserved. No portion of this book may be reproduced, stored in a retrieval system, or transmitted in any form or by any means—electronic, mechanical, photocopy, recording, scanning, or any other—except for brief quotations in critical reviews or articles, without prior written permission from the publisher.

All Scripture quotes are taken from the New International Version of the Bible from Thomas Nelson, (the NIV) unless otherwise noted.

THE HOLY BIBLE, NEW INTERNATIONAL VERSION®, NIV® Copyright © 1973, 1978, 1984, 2011 by Biblica, Inc.™ Used by permission. All rights reserved worldwide.

Scripture taken from the New King James Version®. Copyright © 1982 by Thomas Nelson. Used by permission. All rights reserved.

Scripture quotations marked (TLB) are taken from The Living Bible copyright © 1971. Used by permission of Tyndale House Publishers, Inc., Carol Stream, Illinois 60188. All rights reserved.

This book came to be because two people demonstrated to me each day of my life what it is to honor the life lessons Jesus Christ taught about the home. These two are named Vaughn and Elsie—my mom and dad.

The hallmark of godliness, in my humble view, is *consistency*. That word, in its wide-ranging meaning, is all that was their lives. The Bible describes Jesus, and people who endeavor to follow him, as the people who are leaders in our life.

Hebrews 13:7 and 8 says:
"Remember your leaders, who spoke the word of God to you. Consider the outcome of their way of life and imitate their faith. *Jesus Christ is the same yesterday and today and forever.*"

My mom and dad were my leaders. I did my best to imitate their faith in God who has proven, through all the years of history, to be the universe's model of consistency and the only Being that can fine tune all in existence, right down to our individual lives … to my life.

My parents played out well the multiple roles demanded of parents, along with one other of supreme importance in my life … my wife. But my parents were my first theological professors long before I faced a prof in a college classroom.

I once wrote in a Theology essay, "I learned the meaning of the mission of Christ early on in life, not through the reading of great authors or even the Scriptures, but from example. For I was too young to be a scholar yet just old enough to be an imitator."

My father, as a minister, was the voice of teaching from the pulpit, the example of ministering to the needs of his congregation and living out the faith of his personal life in front of my eyes in our home, all my days—consistently.

My mother was his helpmeet, not desiring the spotlight, yet partnering in ministry and life with my father. Within the church, and at every level of our lives, they ministered to the people God gave to them—consistently.

They were a team to the point that it was nearly impossible to say one of their names without including the other. Nearly 70 years of marriage will do that to two people.

I could not be more thankful for their heritage—a heritage of love, caring, sharing, godly wisdom, and example. And of course, consistency. I could not be more thankful for the home I grew up in that I lovingly call, my *Leave It to Beaver* life.

Thanks mom and dad for all you have given me, and for tolerating my often not too good an imitation of your lives.

And thank-you most of all for introducing me to Jesus from my very first breath on this earth.

Table of Contents

Preface	7
Introduction	10
Chapter One . . . . What a Family	12
Chapter Two . . . . The Lineage and the Legacy	20
Chapter Three . . . . . . The Legacy	29
Chapter Four . . . . The Family Album	38
Chapter Five . . . . The Family Pecking Order	48
Chapter Six . . . . Humility and the Family	58
Chapter Seven . . . . . Maturity and the Family	69
Chapter Eight . . . . . . The Tongue and the Family	79
Chapter Nine . . . . . . Forgiveness and the Family	89
Chapter Ten . . . . . . Respect and the Family	99
Chanter Eleven . . . . Held Together by Him	113
Chapter Twelve . . . . Perfection in Motion	123
Chapter Thirteen . . . The Joy of Sacrifice	140
Conclusion	147
About the Author	148

PREFACE

Alex Haley, the author of "Roots," once wrote, "In every conceivable manner, the family is a link to our past, and a bridge to our future."

If the family of Jesus is the example, this statement is fully true. Little more can be learned on any and every topic in the world than one that fully includes the life of Christ. A study of his family, and how our family would be positively impacted by such a study, demonstrates completely how a link to a family from the past—in this case, the family of Jesus—creates a bridge to our future. And when that bridge is built upon safety in Christ, it is a bridge worth building.

The plan was for God to come to earth in human form and walk among us, teach us, be a living example, live a sinless life, then allow himself to be offered as the sacrifice—once and for all—to atone for the sin of a broken creation. Consider this Scripture in both the Old and New Testaments:

"Therefore, the Lord himself will give you a sign: The virgin will conceive and give birth to a son and will call him Immanuel" (Isaiah 7:14). By the way, this passage in Isaiah was written over 700 years before the event of Christ's birth.

"The virgin will conceive and give birth to a son, and they will call him Immanuel" (which means "God with us") Matthew 1:23, the fulfillment of the prophecy.

The plan of Jesus coming to earth as God in human form was also to experience *all* the challenges of life that we experience. This plan **had** to include his living within the confines of a family unit. It simply had to be this way.

So much of our life, and the formation of who we are, is created in the literal Petri dish of what *is* our family. Consider this Scripture found in Hebrews 2:17 and 18:

"For this reason he had to be made like them, *fully human in every way*, in order that he might become a merciful and faithful high priest in service to God, and that he might make atonement for the sins of the people. Because he himself suffered when he was tempted, he is able to help those who are being tempted."

So, how can a link to the family of Jesus make a difference in our family unit today and become worthy of our study?

It is simple really.

Because Jesus changes lives wherever he dwells.

The Family of Jesus

Timeless Lessons for Modern Families

INTRODUCTION

Little can be more complex than living in the day-to-day of family life and relationships. For Jesus to be "fully human in every way," he had to have wholly experienced the family. That means Jesus had to be in a *real* family. Not a make-believe, pretend, bogus family. He had to experience all phases and possibilities of bona fide authentic family living like all of us do — warts and all.

Jesus knew what it was to receive the total focus of doting parents. He knew the feeling of being the only child. He knew the experience of a family structure of having a stay-at-home mom and a dad who went to work daily, teaching him the family craft of carpentry ... a little family at peace within their home and community.

He also knew the feeling of family brokenness, dealing with stepbrothers and sisters as Joseph was not his biological father—remember? Luke 1:31 through 35 tells the story as Mary is being told by an angel what is about to happen:

"'You will conceive and give birth to a son, and you are to call him Jesus. He will be great and will be called the Son of the Most High. The Lord God will give him the throne of his father David, and he will reign over Jacob's descendants forever; his kingdom will never end.'
'How will this be,' Mary asked the angel, 'since I am a virgin?'
The angel answered, 'The Holy Spirit will come on you, and the power of the Most High will overshadow you. So the holy one to be born will be called the Son of God.'"

Jesus also knew what it was like to grow up in a single parent household, raised by his mom as, somewhere along the line, he had to deal with the grief of losing his dad. And he knew the pressures of being the oldest and most counted upon, in a family of at least seven kids, with tensions of relational challenge at every turn.
As the Bible recounts—it was crucial for Jesus to know and experience all that is life for us, being "fully human in every way", in order for him to become the "merciful and faithful high priest in service to God" (Hebrews 2:17). This was necessary, so we can have confidence in knowing that he really does relate to

whatever it is that we must face from day-to-day. The family, as a life experience, was going to be a uniquely important part of Jesus being fully human. The family is the one aspect of life all human beings have in common no matter the family description—perfect or imperfect.

The plan began as we begin—born as a helpless baby, learning about life year by year, and the role we are to play as we grow into the person God planned for us to be. He would experience it all. That was God's plan for how His Only Son would save mankind.

Through love.

Through demonstrating that love in a family setting.

Through the creation of a whole new family by means of a loving sacrifice he would eventually make for us all.

Through loving all of humanity into the family of God.

Chapter One

What a Family

"A Family is a circle of strength, founded on faith, joined by love, and kept by God."
~ Unknown

1

In anyone's world, moving toward the realized accomplishment of what one has determined to be the reason for their own existence is often the greatest challenge of life. To face that test without the understanding and support of your family nearly takes the challenge beyond the bounds of achieving. Time and again, we find that those who have an extraordinary calling planted deeply within their soul are among the most misunderstood and least supported by those closest to them.

Florence Nightingale substantially impacted the course of modern nursing and medicine, but if the "Lady with the Lamp" had listened to the objections of her family, it would not have been so. Ms. Nightingale was born into a wealthy British family living in Florence, Italy, in 1820. She expressed her interest in nursing to her parents, going so far as to say she felt a godly calling into the field of medicine. In that period of history, nurses were considered uneducated and even promiscuous. Her parents were immovable and forbade her from pursuing her nursing dream. However, after refusing a marriage proposal, Florence, at age 30, had the self-motivation to enroll into nursing school. Her parents finally gave in when they realized how highly dedicated she was to the field of nursing. Florence Nightingale's career led to improved sanitary conditions at hospitals, developing better nursing practices saving millions of lives, and created educational programs and schools for future opportunity for nurses. And why did she become known as the "Lady with the Lamp"? It was during the Crimean War, that Nightingale gained the nickname "Lady with the Lamp" from a phrase in a report in The Times of London:

"She is a 'ministering angel' without any exaggeration in these hospitals, and as her slender form glides quietly along each corridor, every poor fellow's face softens with gratitude at the sight of her.

When all the medical officers have retired for the night and silence and darkness have settled down upon those miles of prostrate sick, she may be observed alone, with a little lamp in her hand, making her solitary rounds."

—William Russell, Cited in Cook, E. T. (1913). The Life of Florence Nightingale. Vol. 1, p. 237.

When we examine the family of Jesus in Scripture, the descriptions are far from supportive. In fact, the interactions recorded often reflect a lack of understanding and even confrontational behavior toward Jesus and his mission.

The prophetical Messianic prayer found in Psalm 69—of which the disciples quoted Psalm 69:9 in John 2:17—is a passage that seems to properly frame the challenges of Jesus within the four walls of his own home.

It reads:

I am a foreigner to my own family, a stranger to my own mother's children; for zeal for your house consumes me," (Psalm 69:8 and 9).

Scripture offers glimpses of the tension between Jesus and his family as they struggled to understand his divine mission. Their inability to comprehend who Jesus truly is—both as a member of the Godhead and as a son and brother—must have created immense strain.

The strain is evident as ever as Jesus' family launches an effort toward regaining control of what was likely looking to them as circumstances getting very much out of control and beyond their sway. Matthew 12:46-47 opens the story:

"While Jesus was still talking to the crowd, his mother and brothers stood outside, wanting to speak to him. Someone told him, 'Your mother and brothers are standing outside, wanting to speak to you.'"

And why? With no mention of Joseph any longer being with them as husband, father and head of the household, Jesus, as the wise eldest son, was more than likely being held on to very tightly as the main significant force in the home.

It would only make sense that he had become their point of security and family strength. His extraordinary wisdom, influence, and character set him apart, making him no ordinary son or brother.

Further, some of his family were probably embarrassed of what was going on. How is it that our brother, Jesus, is now such an authority on every subject in the universe?! If he was really this smart, why didn't he help me more with my homework? (You know how siblings tend to overstate the obvious.)

Life had become increasingly tense as Jesus' eternal mission was now coming into view for *everyone* to see. He was not about to have a public discourse with his family as to their heightened feelings on the topic of the direction his life was taking, especially as it related to his Father's heavenly business. They were simply not able to understand the greatest reason for his existence on this earth.

Of course, he loved them genuinely and uniquely. But what they were demanding did not allow him to be fully obedient to the will of his Heavenly Father. Therefore, an emotional dialogue was not going to help anyone as he continued to wade more deeply into eternal history. Understanding his role as family member is one thing. Understanding his mission as God/man and Savior of the world is totally another. And reaching that level of understanding was, at least to this point, not going very well at home.

There was a short give and take that, when you contemplate what was behind the words, represented astonishing bitterness and deep seeded feelings of resentment and anger, especially if there was any grasp at all of the dangers that awaited Jesus and his personal safety in the space and time in which they lived.

"After this, Jesus went around in Galilee. He did not want to go about in Judea because the Jewish leaders there were looking for a way to kill him. But when the Jewish Festival of Tabernacles was near, Jesus' brothers said to him, *'Leave Galilee and go to Judea, so that your disciples there may see the works you do. No one who wants to become a public figure acts in secret. Since you are doing these things, show yourself to the world.'* For even his own brothers did not believe in him" (John 7:1-5).

Something devastatingly caustic was happening within the family of Jesus that brought them to this place where even his own brothers did not believe in him and were more than willing to push him into harm's way. There are lessons to be learned from this family that are relevant for us and all our families today.

Here are some related thoughts through questions I would like for us to consider as we study this family:
- *How did Jesus handle being disrespected by those closest to him—despite his great authority?*
- *How do I respond when I feel disrespected in my own family?*
- *Did their family trouble leave any map of guidance through Scripture for us and our families today?*
- *What can I learn from the way Jesus handled his family tensions as well as tensions with his friends?*
- *What is different—or the same—regarding family brokenness between families of Jesus' day and our families of today?*

In our society, a broken home is, unfortunately, *not* an unusual thing. In fact, that heritage has become more the norm than the unusual.

We immediately think of divorce as the primary contributor to broken homes. However, add to divorce deaths in a family, those off serving in the military, and the hundreds of thousands who have had to face legal issues—whether it is prison, deportations, etc.—and we find that far more are dealing with brokenness in the home than we ever imagined.

In fact, family tragedy through brokenness brings an amazing amount of commonality to this specific conversation. This realization leads one to think that Jesus not only had to experience living in a family to understand being fully human—he had to live in a broken family to gain the full measure of human understanding.

The numbers of broken homes in our land have become far larger than we are able to fully comprehend. It would only make sense that family stresses have always been a part of societies through time, and the relationship strains in the house Jesus grew up in would not have been any different.

Moreover, Jesus' family may have had to deal with exaggerated domestic issues simply because of who Jesus is. Think of the peaks and valleys, the joys and the quandaries, the wonder and the questions that would exist living with one possessing *all* knowledge, *all* power, *all* insight, and by the way, was perfect and sinless in every way.

Think of the pressures as you contemplate living with absolute perfection as a family member. (I can hear some of you say to yourselves, *"What's the big deal? My family lives with perfection every day!"* Really? And now, back to reality.)

On one hand, it would have been a privilege. On the other hand, it would have been a constant reminder of your own glaring imperfections. Consider this Scripture of description as to how Jesus was perfect in every way:

"To this you were called, because Christ suffered for you, leaving you an example, that you should follow in his steps. He committed no sin, and no deceit was found in his mouth. When they hurled their insults at him, he did not retaliate; when he suffered, he made no threats. Instead, he entrusted himself to him who judges justly" (1 Peter 2:21-23).

What an incredible life!

Imagine what literally living with God in the flesh would bring to a family dynamic! Are you picturing this?! You think Clark Kent had a tough time keeping his identity in check with his family and friends! The set of circumstances within the family of Jesus had to have been off the charts.

Yet, Jesus chose to live in a family setting versus life like, say, John the Baptist, who lived as a hermit in the desert.

Why?

Every aspect of Christ's life was for our benefit—a life from which we can learn and draw examples of perfection in human form.

What is it about the family unit that God would have us see and gain understanding from?

The family can only survive, thrive, and truly find itself, if Christ and his life's example, is in the midst of it!

Chapter Two

The Lineage and the Legacy

"If you want to change the world, go home and love your family." ~ Mother Teresa

2

Once upon a time, in a small village nestled between rolling hills, there stood an ancient apple tree in the middle of a modest farm. This tree had been planted by a man named Samuel, the great-grandfather of the current farm owner, Thomas. Samuel had planted the tree with care, nurturing it as he raised his family, and over the years, it had grown tall and sturdy, bearing the most delicious apples the village had ever known.

The apple tree had become a symbol of the family's legacy. It was said that Samuel had planted the tree with a heart full of hope for the future, praying that it would provide for his children and their children after them. And indeed, the tree had done just that. Every autumn, the tree would produce an abundant harvest, and the apples would be sold at the village market, providing for the family's needs.

When Samuel's son, Jacob, inherited the farm, he, too, took great care of the tree. He taught his son, Matthew, how to prune its branches and how to protect it from the harsh winter winds. Jacob often said, "This tree is more than just wood and leaves. It carries our family's hopes, dreams, and hard work. We must take care of it, just as it has taken care of us."

Matthew, in turn, passed on this wisdom to his son, Thomas. But Thomas, unlike his father and grandfather, did not see the same value in the old tree. He was a man of the modern world and believed that the farm would be better off if he cut down the tree to make room for more profitable crops. "The tree is old and takes up too much space," Thomas thought. "It's time for something new."

One day, as Thomas stood by the tree, axe in hand, ready to chop it down, his young daughter, Lily, ran up to him. "Papa, what are you doing?" she asked, her wide eyes full of concern.

"I'm going to cut down this old tree, Lily," Thomas replied. "It's time to make room for something new and more useful."

Lily looked up at the tree, her little face full of sadness. "But Papa, this tree is special! Grandpa told me that Great-Grandpa Samuel planted it a long time ago, and it's been taking care of our family ever since. Please don't cut it down."

Thomas paused, looking at his daughter's pleading face and then at the tree. He remembered the stories his father had told him about the tree's history, about how it had provided for the family through thick and thin. He realized that the tree was not just an old piece of wood standing in the field; it was a living testament to the love, hard work, and perseverance of his ancestors.

Thomas put down the axe and knelt beside Lily. "You're right, Lily," he said, hugging her close. "This tree is special. It's a part of our family, and it deserves to be cared for, just like our ancestors did."

From that day on, Thomas began to see the apple tree in a new light. He taught Lily how to take care of it, just as his father had taught him. And every year, when the tree bore its sweet fruit, Thomas would tell Lily stories of her great-great-grandfather Samuel, who had planted the tree with hope for the future.

The apple tree continued to stand tall on the farm, a symbol of the family's legacy. It reminded each generation of the importance of honoring the past while nurturing the future. And as the tree's roots grew deeper, so did the family's love and respect for the legacy left to them—a legacy that would continue to bear fruit for generations to come.

There is very little we know about the family of Jesus as a whole really. First, the major time gap in Scripture between the age of twelve and the beginning of Christ's ministry at age thirty is well "un"-documented. His earthly father, Joseph, was, without warning, no longer mentioned in the Bible leaving all to simply wonder—what happened to Joseph?

What we *do* know about Joseph was that he was chosen to play the role of head of the household Jesus grew up in—just like Mary was chosen to be his mother. That statement will bother some of you initially, but let's reflect upon the facts for a moment as to the profound importance of Joseph in God's eternal plan.

What we know about Joseph was that he was a strong, Godly, obedient, caring, loving, hardworking, humble, forgiving man and father that raised Jesus well — and according to the wishes of the Heavenly Father. His role as father meshed thoroughly with that of the Heavenly Father in the embodiment of his character, as well as with who Joseph was in an historical timeline.

Consider this:

According to Scripture, it was Joseph who was key to fulfilling prophecy as Jesus being of the house and lineage of David. As supremely important as the virgin Mary was in the birth of Christ, Joseph was just as important to the fulfilling of prophesy and Christ's historical place as Messiah. They were a necessary team. Reflect on this Scripture that introduces us to Mary and Joseph:

"… God sent the angel Gabriel to Nazareth, a town in Galilee, to a virgin pledged to be married to a man named Joseph, *a descendant of David*. The virgin's name was Mary." (Luke 1:26 and 27).

And when it came to giving directives for the new little family, those came through the recognized head of the household — Joseph. Let me give to you a few prime scriptural examples.

    Matthew 1:18-25

[18] This is how the birth of Jesus the Messiah came about: His mother Mary was pledged to be married to Joseph, but before they came together, she was found to be pregnant through the Holy Spirit. [19] Because Joseph her husband was faithful to the law, and yet did not want to expose her to public disgrace, he had in mind to divorce her quietly.

[20] But after he had considered this, an angel of the Lord appeared to him in a dream and said, "Joseph son of David, do not be afraid to take Mary home as your wife, because what is conceived in her is from the Holy Spirit. [21] She will give birth to a son, *and you are to give him the name Jesus*, because he will save his people from their sins."

[22] All this took place to fulfill what the Lord had said through the prophet: [23] "The virgin will conceive and give birth to a son, and they will call him Immanuel" (which means "God with us").

[24] When Joseph woke up, *he did what the angel of the Lord had commanded him* and took Mary home as his wife. [25] But he did not consummate their marriage until she gave birth to a son. *And he gave him the name Jesus.*

Matthew 2:13-15

[13] When they had gone, an angel of the Lord appeared to Joseph in a dream. "Get up," he said, "take the child and his mother and escape to Egypt. Stay there until I tell you, for Herod is going to search for the child to kill him."

[14] So he got up, took the child and his mother during the night and left for Egypt, [15] where he stayed until the death of Herod. And so was fulfilled what the Lord had said through the prophet: "Out of Egypt I called my son."

And Matthew 2:19-23

[19] After Herod died, an angel of the Lord appeared in a dream to Joseph in Egypt [20] and said, "Get up, take the child and his mother and go to the land of Israel, for those who were trying to take the child's life are dead." [21] So he got up, took the child and his mother and went to the land of Israel. [22] But when he heard that Archelaus was reigning in Judea in place of his father Herod, he was afraid to go there. Having been warned in a dream, he withdrew to the district of Galilee, [23] and he went and lived in a town called Nazareth. So was fulfilled what was said through the prophets, that he would be called a Nazarene.

Joseph was entrusted by God to both hear and obey, as well as use good judgement as head of the household, for protection of his wife and son. The family to which God place His only begotten son had a well-defined structure in lineage as well as its own internal hierarchy. And God honored it all.

Joseph and Mary were chosen by God as a team, just as every mom and dad in every marriage in every home becomes a team as they take vows before God and witnesses, exchanging rings as a promise to one another and—as a statement to all others—that together they have become *one* in the holy establishment of their home. Each had a role to fulfill. Within the framework of that relationship, *make no mistake*, God had and has a plan. And it is God's desire that every portion of that plan be accomplished under his leading and blessing for each family established to this day — in His name.

This may be one of the most important lessons taught us through the family of Jesus! We seem to have forgotten the importance of the family, and the establishing of a blessed home led personally by God. The family of Jesus reminds us.

Here then is God's promise to King David concerning the Messiah coming from his lineage (family) in 2 Samuel 7:12-14, roughly 950 years before the birth of Christ. Make no mistake, his promise, through Jesus is still impacting us today:

"When your days are fulfilled and you rest with your fathers, I will set up your seed after you, who will come from your body, and I will establish his kingdom. He shall build a house for My name, and I will establish the throne of his kingdom forever. I will be his Father, and he shall be My son."

Isn't it interesting, that in all the talk and description of his kingdom and the throne in God's world and plan, it still simply comes down to a house, a Father, parental roles, and a child … a son—the establishment of a family?
And it was all accomplished just as God the Father promised through the lineage of David through Joseph and Mary, and the life of Jesus Christ—the Son!

Here is the prophesy of the lineage of David stated in Isaiah 9:6 and 7 over 700 years before the birth of Christ:

"For unto us a Child is born, Unto us a Son is given; And the government will be upon His shoulder. And His name will be called Wonderful, Counselor, Mighty God, Everlasting Father, Prince of Peace. Of the increase of *His* government and peace *There will be* no end, Upon the *throne of David* and over His kingdom,
To order it and establish it with judgment and justice from that time forward, even forever. The zeal of the LORD of hosts *will* perform this."

And Matthew Chapter One states Joseph's direct role in the fulfillment of that prophesy through the first sixteen verses of the "genealogy of Jesus the Messiah the son of David, the son of Abraham," (Matthew 1:1) beginning with Abraham in verse 2, and culminating with the birth of Christ in verse 16:

"… and Jacob the father of Joseph, the *husband* of Mary, and Mary was the mother of Jesus who is called the Messiah. Thus there were fourteen generations in all from Abraham to David, fourteen from David to the exile to Babylon, and fourteen from the exile to the Messiah."

Yes, Joseph was chosen to be the husband of Mary and the earthly father of Jesus—becoming a team—establishing a uniquely special family.

Every well-established home requires the influence of a strong yet loving father as role model. And Mary was chosen to be his mother as every home requires the gentle yet strong love only a mother can bring. Together, they form the sturdy foundation upon which God can build a home. Put them both together and you have described the full and complete personage of the love of God.

God's plan was for Jesus to be the new Adam and the first of his new family that was to be established in the righteousness and purity of his only Son; the example upon which we can build our homes. Scripture explains it this way:

"So, it is written: 'The first man Adam became a living being'; the last Adam, a life-giving spirit. The spiritual did not come first, but the natural, and after that the spiritual. The first man was of the dust of the earth; the second man is of heaven.

And just as we have borne the image of the earthly man, so shall we bear the image of the heavenly man" (1 Corinthians 15:45-47, 49).

This is what is available to us when we decide to bring the leadership of Christ into our homes, allowing his blessing and calling to become reality. We ourselves not only come to be a new creation—but our homes also. We can, for the sake of our family, bear the image of those that came before us in our family, but also the image of the heavenly man … Jesus. We can reflect his image and example for those that live within our family.

"Therefore, if anyone is in Christ, the **new creation** has come: The old has gone, the **new** is here!" (2 Corinthians 5:17)

What is the family life of Jesus teaching us about our homes as we look at the possibilities of our own specific family legacy?

Understand that your family has a God given legacy, a future plan, through you and your children just like God established through the house of David.

Hard to believe? Maybe. But it is true.

God desires to achieve something uniquely great through you and your children that he can only accomplish through your home and their lives.

Believe it!

Chapter Three

The Legacy

"Legacy. What is a legacy? It's planting seeds in a garden you never get to see."
Lin-Manuel Miranda, playwright

3

Katherine Johnson, born in 1918 in White Sulphur Springs, West Virginia, showed a remarkable talent for mathematics from a young age. Her gift was so extraordinary that she was allowed to skip several grades, and by the age of 10, she was attending high school. Her family, recognizing her potential, made the significant decision to move 120 miles away so Katherine could continue her education, something that was not readily available to African Americans in her hometown.

Katherine graduated from high school at 14 and from college at 18 with degrees in mathematics and French. Despite the barriers of race and gender, she persisted in pursuing her passion for mathematics. Her journey eventually led her to work for NASA, where her mathematical genius would change history.

At NASA, Katherine Johnson's skills in analytical geometry were crucial to the success of some of the United States' most significant space missions, including the first manned flight to the moon. Her calculations were so reliable that astronaut John Glenn famously insisted that she personally verify the numbers for his orbital mission, saying, "If she says they're good, then I'm ready to go."

Katherine's contributions not only cemented her legacy as a pioneer in space exploration but also dramatically impacted her family's legacy. Her story became a source of immense pride and inspiration, not just for her descendants but for countless others who learned of her achievements. Katherine Johnson's life and work shattered racial and gender barriers, opening doors for future generations of women and people of color in STEM (science, technology, engineering, and mathematics) fields.

In our present-day society, for the special accomplishment of each life who lives in your home and family, there is a unique gifting and calling to be fulfilled.

I recently read an anonymously penned thought in the form of a person interviewing God and they asked Him, "What is one of life's lessons you want us Your children to learn?"

God's reply was, "To learn they cannot make anyone love them. All they can do is let themselves be loved by and through me as I give to them direction in life."

Mary and Joseph were to establish a home that would play an important role in the formative years of the life of Jesus, true. But what about his siblings and the call upon their lives?

Every member in the family is important in God's overarching mission for the world. We will delve into this more specifically in later chapters, but we do know that the siblings of Jesus later turned out to be important leaders in the sharing of the Gospel and their testimony as to whom Jesus truly is. Two of his brothers, James, and Jude, wrote books that numbered among those of the New Testament. And James became an important early leader in the church, until his martyrdom, being known as *James the Just*.

In all of God's creation, *nothing* is more important than the home and our family unit!

God made a promise to all of mankind, from the beginning of time, establishing a clear definition of the meaning of family. Isn't it amazing that the safety of our very souls is directly connected to the family. To God the Father, nothing is more sacrosanct than family.

Consider, if you will, this introduction of the account of the first family's line:

"This is the written account of Adam's family line. When God created mankind, he made them in the likeness of God. He created them male and female and blessed them. And he named them "Mankind" when they were created (Genesis 5:1 and 2).

He saved the earth from destruction when he saved Noah—and his family (Genesis 6:18). The promise to Abraham was that he would be the father of the families of the world essentially (Genesis 12:2). God freed the children of Israel through Moses, yes, but his family (his blood family, adopted family, and in-laws) all played unique and special roles as God carried out his plan (Exodus 2:1-10). And our very relationship to God is to him as our Father and we his children—a family.

Nothing is more important to God than the family!

The great finale is that we spend eternity in heaven together where Jesus promised that he was preparing a place for us. In John 14:2 and 3, Jesus tells us:

"My Father's house has many rooms; if that were not so, would I have told you that I am going there to prepare a place for you? And if I go and prepare a place for you, I will come back and take you to be with me that you also may be where I am."

Think for a moment about the way Jesus described heaven. Think about all the grandiose words he could have used to blow us away as he talked about that unbelievably incredible place he knew so very well. Yet, he called it, and described it as, a "house" with rooms. A house with my own room made just for me. My colors. My stuff. "Prepared" for me. I call that a home. And a house becomes a completed home only when a family lives there.

From the beginning of time, through to us today, it has always been about the family. And the family of Jesus is that reminder to us that no matter what trials we face, answers are awaiting us if we strive to keep our families together, working faithfully to strengthen them in his support and wisdom.

On a side note: When we see attacks by the enemy, Satan, on the world, on the Church, on any nation or organization that is doing its best to serve people, his strategy of attack is to weaken that target. And the attack invariably comes by weakening the family structure of that target.

We see this magnified in our own country as an attack is well underway on the strength and moral structure of the family unit whether it is an attack through the governmental and educational leadership of our nation, or a fight for the minds and lives of our children.

It is an attack through weakening the importance of parental guidance and authority. We are under attack at the very heart of the family itself by striking at our children both our born and unborn. The attack is relentless!

We mentioned education, but our children face attack from the games they play, the media they watch and listen to, and through the subliminal and not so subliminal images and messages (some of which are flagrantly pornographic) they carry with them in their pockets on a phone.

Satan knows full well the importance of the family unit. He did his best to war against Christ through his own family, and nothing has changed from that time until now.

Jesus fully understood this to an even greater degree, as we will see he protected his family as a son, a brother, a Savior dying on a cross, and a resurrected Lord coming to deliver healing personal truths.

All long-term success and fulfillment in God's world are through the family—or a setting that emulates the family—positively impacting our lives and beyond.

God's promise to David and his lineage were not restricted to the family of David only. Scripture speaks to the relationship between God and David this way:

"After removing Saul, he made David their king. God testified concerning him: 'I have found David son of Jesse, a man after my own heart; he will do everything I want him to do'" (Acts 13:22).

In that relationship, God made a promise to David that was to impact every human being born to this earth from the moment that promise was made.

Families impact the generations for both the positive and negative. Our families are no exception. We've got to be able to see beyond the immediate and look honestly at the legacy we are leaving for the generations that follow us.

The decisions we make today set into motion events that will reverberate into the generations to come. Think about a decision to be faithful to a spouse that is either admonished or ignored. How would keeping that family together impact the children and their children for years to come? The opposite of that decision is also true.

That is why Scripture having to do with our sins visiting the generations is not so much a judgment of God upon us but rather, more of an issue of spiritual physics. Think in terms of, every action having a reaction. It is our own decisions that become the judgement of our lives. See it in that light when you read Scripture that states:

"Because of their iniquity, and also because of the iniquities of their fathers, they shall rot away like them" (Leviticus 26:39).

Is this the harshness of God? Or the consequence of our own choices? I believe God gets way too much blame for the negatives that surround our lives when it is our own decisions, and the decisions of family members, that are truly to blame for those consequences.

However, decisions made by others, though they may make life a far greater challenge, are not a sentence that is inescapable or necessarily forced upon us. We, with the Lord's help, *have* the power to break such a negative heritage.

It is we ourselves that must determine that in God's strength and wisdom, we are going to change the direction of the decisions made before or around us. Consider then this statement from Scripture:

"The soul who sins shall die. The son shall *not* suffer for the iniquity of the father, nor the father suffer for the iniquity of the son. The righteousness of the righteous shall be upon himself, and the wickedness of the wicked shall be upon himself" (Ezekiel 18:20).

There has to be a moment in time where we as individuals stand up, look at the consequences of ours or other's decisions that have impacted us for the negative, and state our own declaration of independence from that history and heritage. Joshua did. Listen to what that kind of declaration sounds like:

"But if serving the LORD seems undesirable to you, then choose *for* yourselves this day whom you will serve, whether the gods your ancestors served beyond the Euphrates, or the gods of the Amorites, in whose land you are living. But ***as for me and my house***, we will serve the LORD" (Joshua 24:15).

There is a point where we have to make a declaration of our own saying to the Lord, "I lay down this victimhood mentality that I have wrongly bought into. I choose to move forward with you in your forgiving redeeming perfecting power! As for me and my house, we will serve **you** Lord!"

In God's loving power and guidance and the impact of Jesus Christ upon our world, we do not have to live life as a victim but rather, we can choose to live life as a victor.

Chapter Four

The Family Album

"What I love most about my home is who I share it with." ~ Unknown

4

In 1901, the Rockefeller family faced a sudden and tragic loss. William Rockefeller, a successful businessman and father of seven, passed away. His death left his family in mourning, and the responsibility of leading the family fell on the shoulders of his eldest son, John D. Rockefeller Jr., who was just 27 years old at the time.

John D. Rockefeller Jr. had already been involved in his father's business, but now he was thrust into a leadership role far sooner than he had anticipated. Despite the immense pressure, he took on the responsibility with determination and a deep sense of duty to both his family and the legacy his father had built. Under John Jr.'s leadership, the Rockefeller family not only maintained their wealth but expanded it significantly. He continued to grow the family's business empire, which included Standard Oil, and became one of the wealthiest and most influential families in American history. However, it was his philanthropic work that truly set him apart and made a lasting impact on the world.

John D. Rockefeller Jr. believed in using his wealth for the betterment of society. He became a leading figure in philanthropy, donating vast sums of money to various causes, including education, medical research, and the arts. He played a crucial role in the establishment of the Rockefeller Foundation, which funded groundbreaking research in public health and science, and supported the creation of numerous educational institutions.

One of his most notable contributions was the funding and development of Rockefeller Center in New York City, a symbol of American industry and culture. Additionally, he was instrumental in the creation of the United Nations Headquarters, donating the land on which it was built.

John D. Rockefeller Jr.'s leadership not only preserved his family's legacy but also transformed it into a force for global good. His vision and generosity helped shape the 20th century, leaving a lasting impact on the world. His story is a powerful example of how stepping up in the face of loss can lead to extraordinary contributions to both family and society.

We have established that Joseph was the specially chosen earthly father of Jesus, playing a crucial role in this eventual larger family, leaving a profound impact as a father to Jesus and his siblings. However, the Bible abruptly stops mentioning Joseph, leaving us to wonder about his fate. We do know that Joseph was around long enough to father at least six other children, leaving a legacy that ran immeasurably deep as the head of a household.

Jesus is now a member of a single parent household of at least six other children. We do not know what happened and when. We just know that this fine father is—gone. And this young man who Joseph raised, who understands perfect love and the totality of sacrificial giving of oneself and is the oldest son, was now head of this household.

The family reliance upon Jesus must have grown rapidly and ever so deeply after losing a father like Joseph. We know it is not uncommon for an elder son to step responsibly forward should something happen to dad. But for this home to suffer such great loss of a special father like Joseph is one earth shaking challenge. Then to have Jesus, as its daily head and father image, begin to himself step away from his family role as he moved into the earthly portion of his heavenly mission, well, this had to leave a gaping void leading to deeply emotional and fervent responses—again. No wonder the bitterness of uncertainty began to surface in the siblings.

Jesus, most likely, helped raise the children, and was seen by them as more of the leader of the family than simply a brother. This would explain much concerning their inability to easily accept this new way of life he took on in what must have seemed to be a sudden and abrupt manner.

Jesus may well have dedicated many of those 18 "lost" years to make sure his mother and the children were in all manner cared for in preparation for his future.

We do know this however, there seemed to exist a sudden and serious struggle in the few references we have of the family. Yet, the inspirer of *all* Scripture (God himself) simply did not allow the private stories of this family unit to spill out—almost in the protective manner of blurred faces of the children of tragedy, or the rich and famous, seen in public photos today—as this was the personal earthly family of God.

However, things were changing in a major way for this household. And the changes were bringing conflict to the unique dynamic of this family.

One such moment of tenseness and drama happened as the family wanted to speak to Jesus during a time he was going about his Heavenly Father's business. His new responsibilities left them clearly unable to understand. Let's look again to that passage in Matthew 12 as it is a passage that has been hard pressed for an explanation through the generations. The response of Jesus, at first blush, seems a bit harsh and heartless. And a clear struggle to regain some semblance of control in the family role of Jesus was evident from their point of view.

"While Jesus was still talking to the crowd, his mother and brothers stood outside, wanting to speak to him. Someone told him, 'Your mother and brothers are standing outside, wanting to speak to you.' He replied to him, 'Who is my mother, and who are my brothers?' Pointing to his disciples, he said, 'Here are my mother and my brothers. For whoever does the will of my Father in heaven is my brother and sister and mother'" (Matthew 12:46-50).

Factor in the immense and sudden change in the direction of the family—especially where the four sons behind Jesus are concerned—and you can imagine the desperate need to talk things out with their big brother, Jesus.

The four behind Jesus were now needing to take leadership roles in the home as Jesus was deeply amid drastically changing his own personal mission and role. Jesus was preparing those coming up behind him for his leaving their home forever, but he must have been sensing that they were well on their way to being ready to take a next step in their lives, much as he pushes us to take next steps in our lives. He had taken the time to help raise them and prepare them for the future that awaited them. And now it was time for them to move forward into their own world of leadership and calling.

And consider this possibility: When Jesus said, "Here are my mother and my brothers," was Jesus making a not-so-subtle point to *the family* that his disciples seemed to now understand him better in this moment than they? Shouldn't his own family have known him better than anyone on earth?

That response from Jesus would have been a major wake-up call to his family. It seems Jesus was giving them a dose of reality as he was not forsaking them but rather, he was reminding them of who he essentially was, and who they were to him and each other. For surely, they had some understanding of his uniqueness and that they simply could not keep him to themselves forever.

Don't you think that the remarkably incredible family story of how Jesus was born, their fleeing to Egypt to escape death, and the many other family stories only they knew, was told through their house often through the years? Don't you believe that, just as each child had their own memories shared within the family circle, Mary and Joseph wanted to make sure all their children knew how special the calling and hand of protection from God was upon them as a total family?

And don't you suppose that Joseph and Mary made sure they understood that a special place in God's plan for the world included them all?

I must believe this to be the case!

There are times when we, as members of God's family, simply get too comfortable having a place within his family. We become content in trying to keep Jesus all to ourselves instead of allowing him to grow us into what he has envisioned for us. But he will buck against this notion. And when he feels you are ready, he will force you to move forward into the next phase of your life.

Expect it!

He wants you to grow and strengthen yourself personally, within the family of God, and your own family.

We know the names of his brothers. And if the manner in which biblical order was adhered to, the names were given us in order of their age beginning with James, then to Joseph, Judas and Simon; this found in the Book of Mark.

And in that same passage, there is an ever so brief mention that Jesus had some sisters and other relatives living near him, but their names, or any details of their lives, were never shared. Further specifics as to how many sisters he had, and the size of his broader family, is simply not expressly offered.

Here is that passage:

"Jesus left there and went to his hometown, accompanied by his disciples. When the Sabbath came, he began to teach in the synagogue, and many who heard him were amazed.

'Where did this man get these things?' they asked. 'What's this wisdom that has been given him? What are these remarkable miracles he is performing? Isn't this the carpenter? Isn't this Mary's son and the brother of James, Joseph, Judas and Simon? Aren't his sisters here with us?' And they took offense at him. Jesus said to them, 'A prophet is not without honor except in his own town, among his relatives and in his own home.' He could not do any miracles there, except lay his hands on a few sick people and heal them. He was amazed at their lack of faith" (Mark 6:1-6).

There is so much going on here in the family realm of the life of Jesus.

In the previous chapter of Mark Chapter 5, we read about some astonishing miracles performed by Christ. He had cast out demons and restored a man's sanity. He healed a woman from a serious health issue she had been battling for years as she merely touch the hem of his garment. And he raised a little twelve-year-old girl back to life after she had died. This little girl was the daughter of the synagogue leader in that town who had gone to Jesus for help, so he was gaining respect in the region from even certain religious leaders.

You have a sense that he was feeling a momentum that he was hoping would be a major positive in and for his own hometown, as well as for his family that resided there. So, he and his disciples headed back with, what I would imagine to be, realistic yet high expectations. But it just wasn't going to be the outcome he was hoping for as they were lacking a key ingredient that we are about to see impacts every family when life's negatives overwhelm us.

The level of judgement and doubt cast upon Jesus in his hometown is totally stifling—and demonstrates in very clear fashion how life's negative attitudes can spill over beyond the immediate family, even to extended family, friends, and acquaintances.

Imagine this!

God himself was stifled and unable to do great things because of this incredibly negative environment and tone of judgement, harshness, and a lack of belief in him.

Here is a prime example of how these kinds of pressures can bring literal failures to life impacting not only us as individuals, but our entire immediate family. I'll say it again. Even Jesus himself was limited in this extreme atmosphere of negativity.

And his experience led to one of the most quoted statements Jesus ever made:

"A prophet is not without honor except in his own town, among his relatives and in his own home" (Mark 6:4).

Jesus demonstrates to us, through this poignant story, that we must press on and not get discouraged to the point of losing the focus of our life's mission. He did not. He pushed forward because he knew how important the completion of that mission was.

He was deeply grieved at what he could *not* do for them. These were the very people who should have known and understood him best! Yet, his family and friends denied the reality of who he was—to the point that it astounded even him as that passage ends with this thought: *"He was amazed at their lack of faith."*

And most importantly for our family, we must recognize the importance of our home being a *positive* place, a place of growing faith in the Lord and each other, so He can perform the miracles on our behalf and complete our personal callings that he has planned and chosen for us.

However, despite this great disappoint in this moment in time, Jesus displayed his unending commitment to them. Most would have thrown up their hands and said something to the effect of — "I guess I will go where I am appreciated" —

and would have left their family behind. How often do we hear of such stories, and the family bond is broken for a lifetime?

What Jesus did was completely the opposite of what most would do in response to such a publicly devastating and humiliating family moment. In fact, it seems that Jesus' loyalty to his family only deepened, evidenced by his words found in John 6:39, regarding his personal protection and devotedness to his own:

"And this is the will of him who sent me, that I shall lose none of all that he has given me, but raise them up at the last day."

Many think of this Scripture as solely in reference to those who were followers of Jesus, who chose to believe in him. *However, the first of all given him were his own family.* They would always possess this unique place in his heart.

So, what is Jesus teaching us about our own family as we will at times face major setbacks to our goals and dreams?

Never stop protecting those closest to you! And no one is closer to you than your own family — despite any deep disappoints, misunderstandings, and resentments that may arise in your life and relationships.

Remain loyal to those God has on purpose given you, placed in your life as family!

God certainly has remained loyal to you.

Chapter Five

The Family Pecking Order

"You don't choose your family; they are God's gift to you." ~ Desmond Tutu

5

Orville and Wilbur Wright, two brothers from Dayton, Ohio, are famous for inventing the first successful airplane, but their journey to this historic achievement was not without its challenges—especially when it came to their relationship with each other.

As children, Orville and Wilbur were very different in personality. Orville was more adventurous and impulsive, while Wilbur was thoughtful and methodical. Their differences often led to disagreements and tension. They would argue over ideas, methods, and even small matters in their daily lives. These differences were especially pronounced as they began working together on various projects, from printing presses to bicycles.

In the late 1890s, when they started working on the concept of human flight, their differing approaches led to frequent clashes. Wilbur's cautious nature sometimes clashed with Orville's eagerness to try new ideas quickly. At times, their arguments were so intense that they considered giving up their partnership.

However, as they continued their work, the brothers began to realize that their differences were actually a strength. Wilbur's careful planning and Orville's bold experimentation complemented each other, leading to breakthroughs they might not have achieved alone. Over time, they learned to respect each other's contributions and work through their disagreements. Their bond deepened as they recognized the value of their collaboration.

In 1903, their partnership culminated in the first successful powered flight at Kitty Hawk, North Carolina. This achievement was a result of years of hard work, persistence, and, most importantly, their ability to reconcile their differences and work together as a team.

After their historic flight, Orville and Wilbur remained close, becoming not just partners in business but also the best of friends. They continued to work together on aviation projects and supported each other through the challenges and successes that followed. Their relationship became a model of how differences can be overcome and how mutual respect and love can turn sibling rivalry into an unbreakable bond.

The story of the Wright brothers is a testament to the power of family, perseverance, and the ability to find common ground even in the face of significant differences. Their friendship and collaboration not only transformed their relationship but also changed the world forever.

Winding through all of this family dynamic is a particular relationship Jesus had to grapple with in what may well have been the rockiest of all his family relationships—that of the relationship with his next to oldest half-brother, James.

The Bible is gracious to the brothers of Jesus in that no one is directly quoted with regard to some of the more insensitive, even harsh, statements to and about Jesus. It is as though family privacy is being honored—as well as some protection being offered—out of respect and future roles of family members. But there seems to always be a spokesperson and catalyst when it is a group that is confronting an individual. And Scripture may well have pointed to James as playing that role as the oldest and the next son to step up, so to speak.

First, the manner in which Jesus dealt with an individual person's failings, especially those in the inner most circle of his life, was to spend deliberate and frank personal face time with them in order to lovingly redirect, (okay, outright discipline) that person, to reassure, support, share forgiveness for their own sake, and inspire them to a new and better direction in life. We see this with Thomas as he was dealing with extreme doubt as to the resurrection of Christ.

"Now Thomas (called Didymus), one of the Twelve, was not with the disciples when Jesus came. So, the other disciples told him, 'We have seen the Lord!' But he said to them, 'Unless I see the nail marks in his hands and put my finger where the nails were, and put my hand into his side, I will not believe it.' A week later his disciples were in the house again, and Thomas was with them. Though the doors were locked, Jesus came and stood among them and said, 'Peace be with you!' Then he said to Thomas, 'Put your finger here; see my hands. Reach out your hand and put it into my side. Stop doubting and believe.' Thomas said to him, 'My Lord and my God!'" (John 20:24-28)

Notice the strong discipline here as Jesus plainly got to the point— "Stop doubting and believe." (*I seriously wish we could have had a recording of this moment, so we could hear the loving but strong of the voice of the Lord. Wow! What a moment that would have been in history!*)

We especially see this trait after the three denials of Peter.

"Peter replied, 'Even if all fall away on account of you, I never will.'

'Truly I tell you,' Jesus answered, 'this very night, before the rooster crows, you will disown me three times'" (Matthew 26:33 and 34).

Jesus provided three opportunities for Peter to state personally how much he truly loved him, thereby bringing him to verbally cancel out the three blasphemy level failings. In so doing, Peter would not have to live with the horrific denial the rest of his days. Jesus, in this personal appearance after the resurrection, wanted to make sure Peter knew all was well and to give Peter a glimpse of his future, ultimately inspiring him to go on with his life and mission victoriously. But there was the patented strong loving discipline too.

A personal time over breakfast was imperative, placing everyone and everything else on hold until Peter's life was back in order. The account goes like this:

"When they had finished eating, Jesus said to Simon Peter, 'Simon son of John, do you truly love me more than these?'

'Yes, Lord,' he said, 'you know that I love you.'
Jesus said, 'Feed my lambs.'
Again, Jesus said, 'Simon son of John, do you truly love me?'
He answered, 'Yes, Lord, you know that I love you.'
Jesus said, 'Take care of my sheep.'

The third time he said to him, 'Simon son of John, do you love me?' Peter was hurt because Jesus asked him the third time, 'Do you love me?' He said, 'Lord, you know all things; you know that I love you.'
Jesus said, 'Feed my sheep. I tell you the truth, when you were younger you dressed yourself and went where you wanted; but when you are old you will

stretch out your hands, and someone else will dress you and lead you where you do not want to go.'
Jesus said this to indicate the kind of death by which Peter would glorify God. Then he said to him, 'Follow me!'" (John 21:15-19)

At the end, Jesus was basically telling Peter—much as he did Thomas—okay, we have worked through this. All is forgotten. I'm good. Now, walk with me!

How does that relate to how you deal with issues in your family when someone lets you or the family down? I would dare say that most make things worse by holding grudges and struggling with unforgiveness — never mind saying all the wrong things in response to the situation.

Jesus demonstrates to us that it is best to forgive, reembrace the one you love, and move on with life together.

Of the four brothers of Jesus, there is only one reference in Scripture to that of Christ's appearing in a one-on-one moment with any of them after His resurrection. That appearance was to James—another indication that it probably *was* James who was verbally struggling in his relationship with big brother.

So, what does that appearance tell you? Jesus was going to lovingly redirect (discipline), reassure, support, share forgiveness for James' own sake, and inspire him to a new and better direction in life, moving on together with him. That appearance is found in I Corinthians 15:3-7 in an account from Paul:

"For what I received I passed on to you as of first importance: that Christ died for our sins according to the Scriptures, that he was buried, that he was raised on the third day according to the Scriptures, and that he appeared to Peter, and then to the Twelve. After that, he appeared to more than five hundred of the brothers at the same time, most of whom are still living, though some have fallen asleep. *Then he appeared to James*, then to all the apostles, and last of all he appeared to me also, as to one abnormally born."

One can only speculate as to what their time together was like at that appearing. However, if we use what we know about how all transpired with Thomas and Peter, it was likely a time of gentle acceptance, an unspoken yet powerful moment of forgiveness—of course followed by a challenge that inspired James through a focused strong brotherly love. Something like … "Stop doubting and believe! Believe I love you and always have! Believe in what we can do together"

Could it have been mutually emotional? Most likely so as this moment has remained extremely private from the rest of us to this day. We have an account of the interaction with Thomas and Peter, but not of this moment with James. These were brothers! This was a private family meeting.

This meeting with James was likely more kin to the emotion Jesus displayed with Lazarus. John 11:32-36 gives us this parallel regarding the emotion of Jesus with those he loved intimately:

"When Mary reached the place where Jesus was and saw him, she fell at his feet and said, 'Lord, if you had been here, my brother would not have died.' When Jesus saw her weeping, and the Jews who had come along with her also weeping, he was deeply moved in spirit and troubled. 'Where have you laid him?' he asked. 'Come and see, Lord,' they replied. **Jesus wept**. Then the Jews said, *'See how he loved him!'*"

The moment with James was to become a major breakthrough of a rekindled relationship of mutual acceptance between two brothers that had gone through serious strain in recent times.

Of course, there was going to exist strong emotion!

Encouragement and personal insight would have also accompanied the emotion that clearly inspired James (like Peter) to emerge as one of the greatly trusted leaders of his day, by both Jew and Roman, becoming known as *James the Just*, as purported to be named by **Hegesippus** (Ἅγιος Ἡγήσιππος) (c. 110 — c. April 7, 180 AD), a Christian chronicler of the early Church.

The growing spiritual maturity of James is seen demonstrated through his letters that define what personal maturity looks like. He willfully received instruction straight from the hand of God.

James was teachable, and eventually wrote concerning particular life topics in which he himself experienced impactful change. He wrote in the authority of God, with himself as the corroborative witness, to the changing power of the first-hand familiarity and example of Jesus: as a brother and as a Savior.

When considering the Book of James in the Bible, could it be that what James desired to share with us is from a clear standpoint of unprecedented personal deliverance and overcoming that he uniquely lived through as a member of Christ's own family? And more importantly—that his brother Jesus never gave up on their relationship however challenging it had become.

Here are a couple of tremendously significant points Jesus desires us to learn regarding ourselves and our families.

First, he desires to spend deliberate one-on-one facetime with you in order to lovingly redirect and discipline you—to make you stronger and more effective in your own life and future, and to make you an even greater asset to your family.

When he does this, Jesus will help you honestly face the real-life issues that have challenged you; yet he will reassure, support, and share forgiveness with you, to inspire you to a new and better direction in life. He loves you that much!

Next, he will show you privately his love and patience in his continued building of all he envisions you to be.

Don't give up on loving your family through the same process toward seeing each member grow in the wisdom and love of Christ! In those times of deep family give and take, and the setting of things straight relationally, exchange these moments in private as Jesus did through example and graciously does with you.

The privacy of reassurance, support, and forgiveness is the greatest demonstration of love and respect we could ever offer—and be offered.

One of my favorite moments in Scripture is found in 1 Corinthians 13, known by many as the Love Chapter. The Bible tells us that God himself is love:

"Whoever does not love does not know God, because God is love" (1 John 4:8).

I personally believe that 1 Corinthians 13:4-8a is a literal description of the personality of God himself and it reads:

1 Corinthians 13:4-8 in the New International Version (NIV) reads:

"Love is patient, love is kind. It does not envy, it does not boast, it is not proud. It does not dishonor others, it is not self-seeking, it is not easily angered, it keeps no record of wrongs. Love does not delight in evil but rejoices with the truth. It always protects, always trusts, always hopes, always perseveres. Love never fails."

What a powerful passage of beautiful insight as to what God our Father is really like! And the moment in that set of verses that we simply must take into our family settings when we face relational difficulties on any and all levels is the phrase that speaks of genuine love saying:

"… it is not easily angered; it keeps no record of wrongs."

What a life changing attribute to introduce into the ambiance of our family. The tone of such beauty begins in the Spirit of Christ and moves into your home through you.

Chapter Six

Humility and the Family

"Family—Where life begins, and love never ends." ~ Unknown

6

Nelson Mandela was born into a royal family in the Eastern Cape of South Africa. His mother had become a devout Christian and she made sure he was educated at a Methodist mission school located close to the palace. When Mandela went away to a Methodist mission secondary school, his guardians were Christians. He attended church every Sunday with them, and Christianity became a significant part of his life. At university he joined the Student Christian Association and led Bible studies for his colleagues.

Mandela became a lawyer and founding member of the ANC Youth League. Unlike many of his activist colleagues he refused to join the ZA Communist Party because he did not agree with its atheism. The white-led ZA government in 1948 moved significantly in a direction of hardening attitudes and passing dozens of laws to reinforce the policy of racial separateness. Mandela and his colleagues stepped up their actions to reverse this dreadful new form of governing. Mandela was eventually sentenced to life imprisonment on charges of sabotage and conspiracy to overthrow the government, only just escaping the death penalty.

Nelson Mandela spent 27 years in prison for his role in fighting a brutal system of racial segregation and oppression called apartheid. During his imprisonment, he was subjected to harsh conditions, including forced labor, isolation, and humiliation by the guards. Despite this, Mandela determined to choose a path of humility that not only helped heal his own spirit but also laid the foundation for healing a deeply divided nation.

While at Robben Island, Mandela was initially filled with anger and bitterness toward his captors. However, over time, he realized that carrying hatred in his heart would only poison his spirit and undermine his struggle for justice.

Instead of allowing himself to be consumed by bitterness, Mandela chose to practice humility. He treated the prison guards with respect and dignity, even when they showed him none in return. He learned their languages, talked to them about their families, and even shared with them the reasons behind his fight against apartheid.

Mandela's humility had a profound impact on those around him. Some of the guards who initially despised him began to see him as a human being and respected him for his dignity and resolve. Over time, this mutual respect grew into genuine relationships, and some of these very jailers would later become his allies in the fight for a peaceful and democratic South Africa.

When Mandela was finally released in 1990, he could have sought revenge against those who had wronged him. Instead, he chose the path of forgiveness and reconciliation. His personal humility allowed him to lead his country, as president of South Africa, to become a global symbol of reconciliation, through a peaceful transition from apartheid to democracy. Mandela's ability to forgive and to reach out to his former enemies was a powerful example that inspired millions and helped heal the wounds of a nation.

Two of his most famous quotes were of him saying:

"I look upon Jesus Christ as the Son of God, as God himself," and, "Until I changed myself, I could not change others."

Mandela's story is a testament to the power of humility.

His willingness to put aside his pride, to forgive those who had wronged him, working for the greater good that brought healing not just to himself, but to an entire nation. His legacy is a reminder that true strength lies not in holding onto anger, but in letting it go and choosing to act with love and compassion.

In the Book of James, Chapter One, James' very first and most immediate words are cloaked in a totally humble self-introduction. He referenced himself simply as, "James, a servant of God and of the Lord Jesus Christ."

From this self-introduction, we would never have known he was the brother of Jesus.

He had every right to introduce himself as, "James, the brother of our Lord." Yet, that moniker seemed to be nowhere near the heart of James. Knowing Jesus as intimately and honestly as he did reinforce the only position he could have reckoned within himself. And that was a position of genuine *humility*.

Jesus is God in his perfect, yet human, form! How *could* we think too highly of ourselves after deeply experiencing him?! The truth of the matter is—we can't.

James was referred to only once in Scripture in the manner of—brother of the Lord, and that was by the Apostle Paul in Galatians 1:18 and 19 when he stated:

"Then after three years, I went up to Jerusalem to get acquainted with Peter and stayed with him fifteen days. I saw none of the other apostles—only James, the Lord's brother."

At the bottom of disputes—especially family disputes—is always a sentiment in which someone is convinced they have been wronged, overlooked, belittled, mistreated, or simply not appreciated and understood. Certainly, James and his siblings might well have had to deal with such issues and feelings.

Being a sibling of Jesus, the Messiah and Promised One himself, would not have been easy for anyone, no matter how strong an effort Christ made to be sensitive to the needs of his family members.

The words of Jesus in Matthew 11:6 seemed to encompass all he had a personal relationship with. He knew full well how colossal his mission was to conquer and bring to full subjugation the powers of sin and death—and the warring evil behind them. Jesus knew that the tactics of the evil one, Satan, is to lead the world to hate him and those associated with him. Jesus understood the difficulty of living with him through his mission and beyond.

Consider his words as he said,

"Blessed is anyone who does not stumble on account of me" (Luke 7:23).

Imagine the attention, good bad or otherwise, that was flooding their family door. There was now this gang of followers that monopolized his time when just prior they, his family, were the probable center of his life. There had to exist the gambit of emotions among the at least six younger siblings of various ages that consisted of feelings of hurt, misunderstanding, and a sense of being left behind, due to all the attention their big brother was now *giving* to these "outsiders", as well as a possible jealousy at all the attention Jesus was *receiving* from these strangers.

In our very human existence of believing we are *the center of the universe*, this had to have been an experience that was extremely hard to swallow; especially when you consider his family seemed to have had Jesus all to themselves for the better portion of that lost 18-year span just prior to the three years of Christ's ministry. Lashing out in some manner was going to come … it was inevitable … and it came.

James, in this set of personal letters we know simply in Scripture as, *the Book of James*, knew what it was to fight a personal battle over a supreme focus on *self*. And from that conflict, James fully understood the casualties that arise out of detonating the armed weapons of words in anger.

As he looked back in reminiscence upon how he was unable to support his own brother, Jesus, during the most treacherous yet important time in the personal history of Jesus himself to and for mankind, James was sure to have felt strongly to *not* attach himself to a legacy and ministry he had not embraced—especially through the positioning of himself in his writings as "the brother of our Lord."

Personally, James had to come to grips with the late timing of his finally recognizing and admitting to whom his brother really and truly is—the Savior of the world! And in all of this, James would now have to make some personal determinations as to how to proceed with this new realization.

It is true that he was now reconciled with Jesus through their personal time together after the resurrection, but imagine the emotional flow given the memories of what he had said, both to the face of Jesus, and behind his back.

James had to find a way to file those memories away that may have even consisted of wishing his own brother harm during his angry frustration. And then the harm came. The memories of his own actions and words were most likely trying to fight their way into James' thought life. Of course, that would only be a natural human phenomenon to have to deal with.

So, in dealing with the reality of who Jesus is, and the humility that must emerge in his presence, there are specific directions this response would take. And we find the thought process of James have made their way into both theology and everyday life as we learn to deal with the serious personal event of failing a loved one.

First, to understand this deep seeded emotion, we need to ask a few questions. Let's begin with the most basic question of all: What does real heartfelt humility look like?

Let me give you the supreme example.

Consider this passage in Philippians 2:2-8, as a definition for all time, as to what real humility is. It is here we find Jesus personified through these inspired words as our example for living in all facets of life—especially our family life:

"Do nothing out of selfish ambition or vain conceit. Rather, in *humility* <u>value others above yourselves</u>, *not looking to your own interests but each of you to the interests of the others.*

<u>*In your relationships with one another, have the same mindset as Christ Jesus*</u>:

Who, being in **very nature God**,
 *did not consider equality with God something **to be used to his own advantage***;

> rather, *he made himself nothing*
>> by taking the very nature of a *servant*,
>> being made in human likeness.

> And being found in appearance as a man,
>> he *humbled himself*
>> by becoming *obedient* to death—
>>> even death on a cross!"

So, what does real humility look like? It looks like—and is embodied in—all that is the life of Jesus.

Humility "values others above yourself."

Humility willingly pushes the interests of others in front of your own.

Humility cannot co-exist with "selfish ambition or vain conceit" any more than light and darkness can occupy the same space.

Humility will cause you to "take the very nature of a **servant**."

Humility will indeed change your "mindset" toward the nature of your relationships with all others, especially those closest to you—your family.

64

And true humility brings you and me to a point of "obedience" to the direction the Lord is leading regarding our words and actions with all others; whatever sacrifice is demanded.

Humility is not just a position of action in a particular setting of circumstance. It is a new personality creation, made by God himself within us, as we allow his influence to emerge through all that **we are—all that we do and say—changing** us fully as we live our lives.

Humility itself is an attribute of God that we are unable to generate in and of ourselves—by ourselves.

Can we create an adequate substitute that makes us look like "good" people, understanding people, even tolerant people? I believe so—**for a time at least, for a specific response needed, and for an immediate result.**

But make no mistake, this is a false humility. If we do not seek the genuine gift from God through our allowing him to change us as we willingly obey his desires in all aspects of our lives, we will never be able to offer others lasting and genuine responses fully clothed in humility.

In saying this, I believe there is a direct interchanging and mirroring between humility and repentance, humility and caring, humility and genuine love.

In the imperfection of our humanity, being willing to face our shortcomings and failures, asking forgiveness of our Heavenly Father and those around us, is necessary to strengthen our position and experience the maturing of our life relationships. It takes a repentant, caring, loving heart to seek that forgiveness, and a heart of humility to recognize the need of it, and then to accept it.

Remember, I mentioned that there were multiple directions our emotions could travel as we deal with our failures.

We can repent of them, asking God to forgive us and give us wisdom in reconciling whatever it is we are facing and with whom we are facing it. Or we can seek to find a shield for ourselves through the justification of our actions, thereby placing ourselves and our actions first in priority above all others.

This response is the opposite of humility leading toward the dangers and pitfalls of arrogance.

Arrogance is a false assessment of oneself as we rationalize our behaviors.

Whereas humility is a truthful assessment of oneself, being willing to look honestly at our shortcomings, coming face to face with what needs to be done as we make an episode of life right in God's eyes and in the lives of others.

A humble heart is one of a repentant contrite spirit seeking forgiveness and *restitution* with anyone we have wronged. Whereas, a false seeking of humility is based upon either an arrogant position of denial, or living in guilt, eventually becoming a life of penance that never fulfills our troubled heart or genuinely brings about genuine lasting resolution. 2 Corinthians 7:10 states strongly:

[10] Godly sorrow brings repentance that leads to salvation and leaves no regret, but worldly sorrow brings death.

True humility is an outgrowth of a servant's heart. Remember the description of the humility of Christ in Philippians Chapter 2? A servant's heart is based upon genuine love. In the words of Jesus,

"Greater love has no one than this: to lay down one's life for one's friends" (John 15:13).

It is willing sacrifice for the wellbeing of another.
So, it is imperative to understand that false humility will show itself in either a form of arrogance, or a life of guilt that never renders resolve.

One avenue becomes extremely secular, never considering God's leading as it is immersed in self. The other leads to a misguided religiosity that is hoping that false sacrifice, versus genuine forgiveness, will find its way to answers and fulfillment.

It is only true humility that has changed the world through the life, message, and ultimate personal sacrifice of Jesus Christ.

It is only the humility of Christ living in you that will change you, your relationships, and your household.

When we contemplate our sin, and treatment of the one who gave so much for us, the same conclusion of finding our way to that place of total humility is all that is left to us. Just like James, we don't feel worthy to be called his brother. Being a servant is all we dare aspire to.

And yet, as with his reconciliation with James, Jesus lets us know that he sees us differently than we see ourselves. He reminds us that we *are* his family, and his father our Father. We are the very ones he sacrificed everything for, saying of us that in all the power of the Father and himself, he would not lose one, but raise us all up at the last day. (John 6:39)

This is the next important thing for us to learn as we consider the story of the family of Jesus:

God will enable you to face your shortcomings honestly when the challenges of life demand it; empowering you to deal with others in Christ-like love, caring, protection, and genuine humility.

Chapter Seven

Maturity and the Family

"A little progress every day adds up to big results." ~ Unknown

7.

George Müller, a Christian evangelist and the director of the Ashley Down orphanage in Bristol, England, is one of history's most remarkable examples of how the prayer of a righteous person can change the world.

Born in 1805 in Prussia (modern-day Germany), Müller was not always the devout man he came to be. In his early years, he lived a life of indulgence, dishonesty, and rebellion. However, in his early twenties, Müller experienced a profound conversion to Christianity, which completely transformed his life. He became deeply committed to living a life of faith, trusting in God for every need.

In 1834, Müller moved to Bristol, England, where he felt called to care for the many orphans living in desperate conditions. At that time, the city was home to thousands of children who had lost their parents to disease or poverty. These orphans roamed the streets, hungry and without hope. Moved by their plight, Müller decided to open an orphanage, but he resolved to do so in a way that would demonstrate the power of prayer and faith in God.

Müller made a bold decision: he would never ask anyone directly for financial support. Instead, he would pray to God for all the needs of the orphanage, trusting that God would provide. He believed that by doing so, he could show the world that God is faithful, and that prayer is powerful.

And so began a life of extraordinary faith and answered prayers. Over the next several decades, Müller cared for over 10,000 orphans, built multiple orphan houses, and distributed millions of gospel tracts and Bibles—all without ever directly asking for a penny from anyone. Every meal, every article of clothing, every brick in the orphanage buildings was provided through prayer.

One of the most famous stories about Müller involves a day when the orphanage had no food for breakfast. The children were seated at the tables, and the staff stood ready, but there was nothing to eat. Müller prayed, thanking God for the food that they were about to receive, even though none was in sight. At that moment, there was a knock on the door. It was the local baker, who had been moved in the night to bake extra bread for the orphanage. Shortly after, the milkman knocked as well—his cart had broken down in front of the orphanage, and he offered the milk to the children since it would spoil otherwise. The children had a full breakfast, just as Müller had prayed.

This was just one of countless instances where Müller's prayers were answered in miraculous ways. His unwavering faith inspired many and demonstrated the power of prayer in a tangible, life-changing way. He kept meticulous records of the donations he received and the specific prayers he prayed, leaving behind a detailed account of God's provision.

Müller's story is not just one of personal devotion but of global impact. His work in caring for orphans set a new standard for charitable work and influenced the establishment of orphanages around the world. Moreover, his example of faith and reliance on prayer continues to inspire Christians globally. His life serves as a powerful reminder that the prayer of a righteous person is indeed powerful and effective, capable of changing not only individual lives but the world at large.

Through his faith and prayer, George Müller not only changed the lives of thousands of orphans in 19th-century England but also left a lasting legacy of what it means to trust in God and live a life committed to prayer. His life story stands as a testimony to the profound impact that one person's prayers can have on the world.

In the Book of James, Chapter One verses 2 through 5, James gives us a specific road map to spiritual *maturity*. He also gives us a hint as to what was shared, recognized, and learned in that most private, post resurrection, appearance between himself and his big brother, Jesus.

Jesus evidently could not get through to James prior to the heightening of events that was his fast-paced three years of ministry—leading to the end of his life on a cross. Due to the animosity existing between them as brothers, James seemed to have a preconceived notion as to what the personal agenda of Jesus was—having nothing to do with Christ's heavenly mission of eventual selfless sacrifice.

James, and the brothers, were convinced that the personal agenda of his older brother was to become, "… a public figure" (John 7:4).

James later wrote:

"Consider it pure joy, my brothers, whenever you face trials of many kinds, because you know that the testing of your faith develops perseverance. Perseverance must finish its work so that you may be *mature* and complete, not lacking anything. If any of you lacks wisdom, he should ask God, who gives generously to all without finding fault, and it will be given to him."

James is the voice of first-hand knowledge to the fact that when life's experiences are lived out in the wisdom and leadership of the Lord, we can persevere to the finish line where godly maturity and fulfillment awaits us.

We can endure only if we rely upon the wisdom granted to us by the Father, rather than trying to manufacture our own wisdom rooted in nothing more than the ignorance created within the realm of limited human knowledge.

Few circumstances in life are tougher than that of deeply entrenched family disputes. And nothing is more disastrous to our lives than endeavoring to deal with family disputes within the confines of our own limited wisdom and lack of understanding.

Only God's insight can keep us on track when family difficulties arise. And the way we tap into God's insight is to again follow the example of Jesus and seek the Father's leading through prayer.

This statement made by James tells us that he witnessed the effectiveness of prayer. Would it be far-fetched to believe that some of that effective prayer was from within his own family? He wrote:

"... The prayer of a righteous person is powerful and effective" (James 5:16b)

I believe that Jesus did not begin his in-depth life of prayer suddenly as he started the trek of his three-year ministry. His prayer life was most likely a hallmark of his entire life beginning as a young boy as this was his source of wisdom and strength, and favor with God. His prayer life and walk with God was most likely witnessed by his family as well. Consider this Scripture in Luke Chapter Two:

"Every year Jesus' parents went to Jerusalem for the Festival of the Passover. When he was twelve years old, they went up to the festival, according to the custom. After the festival was over, while his parents were returning home, the boy Jesus stayed behind in Jerusalem, but they were unaware of it. When they did not find him, they went back to Jerusalem to look for him. After three days they found him in the temple courts, sitting among the teachers, listening to them and asking them questions. *Everyone who heard him was amazed at his understanding and his answers.* When his parents saw him, they were astonished. And Jesus grew in wisdom and stature, and in favor with God and man" (Luke 2:41-43, 45-48a, 52).

Developing a relationship with God through prayer is paramount to our gaining an understanding of God's ways and path for us.
If you are a parent, teach your children when they are young to pray so they are comfortable to pray as though they are having a conversation with God. If you do this with and for them, you will find their approach to life is unlike the way others handle living.

The Bible tells us that God's will for our living is to be happy through contentment as we seek God's answers to all our issues of life—being thankful because he will make all things work together for our good. Here are some scriptural thoughts for you and your family to consider:

"These are the things you are to teach and insist on. If anyone teaches otherwise and does not agree to the sound instruction of our Lord Jesus Christ and to godly teaching, they are conceited and understand nothing. They have an unhealthy interest in controversies and quarrels about words that result in envy, strife, malicious talk, evil suspicions and constant friction between people of corrupt mind, who have been robbed of the truth and who think that godliness is a means to financial gain.

But godliness with contentment is great gain" (1 Timothy 6:2b-6).

"Rejoice always, pray continually, give thanks in all circumstances; for this is God's will for you in Christ Jesus" (1 Thessalonians 5:16-18).

"And we know that in all things God works for the good of those who love him, who have been called according to his purpose" (Romans 8:28).

In the example of Jesus, we must seek the leading of our Father in heaven by finding a way to focus deeply, not only on our praying, but also upon gaining his answers through listening.

Jesus prayed when he knew others would not normally be around, often early in the morning or through the night. And we know that the bigger the decisions he had to make, the longer he prayed over and through those issues.

"One of those days Jesus went out to a mountainside to pray, and spent the night praying to God. When morning came, he called his disciples to him and chose twelve of them, whom he also designated apostles" (Luke 6:12, 13).

Choosing his team was an all-important task as these were to be the apostles that would take the message of God's love to the world—all having to face the tests of life and death, and all but one of the original twelve having a massive impact on what was to become known as, Christianity.

Just a note: *God has chosen your team and made them your family.*

Jesus also knew his prayers would be answered. This is the Prayer of Jesus as he prepared to raise Lazarus from the dead:

"Then Jesus said, 'Did I not tell you that if you believe, you will see the glory of God?' So, they took away the stone. Then Jesus looked up and said, 'Father, I thank you that you have heard me. I knew that you always hear me, but I said this for the benefit of the people standing here, that they may believe that you sent me'" (John 11:40-42).

And Jesus knew he was not alone in his praying.

"In the same way, the Spirit helps us in our weakness. We do not know what we ought to pray for, but the Spirit himself intercedes for us through wordless groans. And he who searches our hearts knows the mind of the Spirit, because the Spirit intercedes for God's people in accordance with the will of God" (Romans 8:26 and 27).

One thing we know for sure is that difficulties will come as the enemy will battle us where we are most vulnerable—with the people we value and rely upon the most—our family.

James then delivers a testimony to the fact that there was no finger pointing or fault finding when he finally allowed Jesus to approach him; only the gifting of what was needed to "be mature and complete, not lacking anything."
He probably rehearsed the words endlessly as to what he *should have* said to Jesus when he had the opportunity—before he lost his brother to a cruel death. But now it was too late.

Then suddenly, to his total astonishment, he had another chance. Another opportunity to lay his heart bare through the unexpected event of Christ's resurrected personal appearance. I wonder if Jesus came to James as Lord, or as his brother? Most likely—both.

Let's imagine the dialogue of James to Jesus in that moment:

"I can't believe I have this chance to tell you how sorry I am that I made your life more difficult than what it was already! I know I was drowning in the selfish feelings that life just wasn't fair. And honestly, I simply wanted you to hear me speak out loud my hurt and pain! I have been so weak—unable to make any good decision or ever say the right thing. I even tried to turn our family against you by talking about you behind your back. Look at the way I treated you—my brother! I thought you wronged us—wronged me! But you never did anything but love us and do your best for us. I realize that now. How could you ever forgive me? Will you please tell me you understand and that we are okay as brothers?"

And into that believing heart of repentance, Jesus poured in. James received the gift of an incredible measure of love from his *brother*, and forgiveness as *Lord*. And from that moment, James own life was resurrected into wisdom, and a road map, and the strength toward *maturity* that indeed allowed him to persevere to the end, and to impact the generations, to follow in his writings what he learned from experiencing the example of the perfection of Jesus as a personal member of the family of Christ.

James learned first-hand that these gifts came to him without a hint of finding fault toward him during his time of personal struggle. But now, he held the realization in his hands that what he was given was worth all that struggle.

James was now able to write an amazing declaration in verse 12 of Chapter One when he penned:

"Blessed is the man who perseveres under trial, because when he has stood the test, he will receive the crown of life that God has promised to those who love him."

This is another important thing Jesus desires us to learn from his family and give a place of consideration to in our own families:

Realize that living with your family through the years is a continual process of maturing.

That process is called, perseverance.

We are only able to persevere when we are able to offer forgiveness in God's love, dealing with each other through God's gift of wisdom.

Remember, James defined the end product of perseverance as, *maturity*.

That end product of maturity, through the effort of growing at a personal level through determined perseverance, is one of the greatest gifts we could ever share with one another as family members.

Don't give up!

Chapter Eight

The Tongue and the Family

"Loud thoughts—Quiet mouth." ~ Mothers Everywhere

8

During the American Civil War, President Abraham Lincoln faced numerous challenges, both on the battlefield and within his own administration. One of the most difficult relationships he had was with his Secretary of War, Edwin Stanton.

Stanton was known for his fiery temper and sharp tongue. He was also openly critical of Lincoln, at times even ridiculing him behind his back. Stanton once referred to Lincoln as a "low-cunning clown" and "the original gorilla." Many of Lincoln's advisors suggested that Stanton should be dismissed from his position due to his disrespectful behavior.

However, Lincoln, who was known for his patience and wisdom, chose a different approach. Instead of reacting to Stanton's insults or seeking revenge, Lincoln remained calm and chose to listen. He recognized Stanton's immense capabilities and his dedication to the Union cause. Lincoln valued Stanton's expertise and knew that he was the best person to manage the war effort, despite their differences.

Lincoln practiced being slow to speak and quick to listen, even in the face of personal attacks. He often visited Stanton's office late at night to discuss military strategies, not allowing Stanton's harsh words to cloud his judgment. Over time, Stanton came to deeply respect Lincoln, recognizing the president's greatness not just as a leader, but as a man.

When Lincoln was assassinated in April 1865, Stanton was by his side. It was Stanton who famously said, "Now he belongs to the ages," as Lincoln passed away. The man who once derided Lincoln now mourned him as one of the greatest leaders the world had ever known.

This story is a powerful testament to the value of being slow to speak and quick to listen. Lincoln's patience and willingness to see beyond Stanton's harsh words allowed him to keep a brilliant mind in his cabinet, which ultimately contributed to the Union's victory in the Civil War. It also led to a profound transformation in their relationship, turning animosity into deep respect and admiration.

A compelling piece of evidence suggesting that James was the source of the harsh words directed at Jesus within their family is the profound impact of Christ's influence on his life. This transformation is evident in his epistles, known as The Book of James in the Bible. In these letters, he instructs all of humanity on the perils of the unbridled tongue and underscores the importance of measured speech. Consider the words he wrote found in James 1:19 and 20:

"My dear brothers, take note of this: Everyone should be quick to listen, slow to speak and slow to become angry, for man's anger does not bring about the righteous life that God desires."

Or these thoughts:

"If anyone considers himself religious and yet does not keep a tight rein on his tongue, he deceives himself and his religion is worthless" (James 1:26).

Or these powerful words in James 3:3-11:

"When we put bits into the mouths of horses to make them obey us, we can turn the whole animal. Or take ships as an example. Although they are so large and are driven by strong winds, they are steered by a very small rudder wherever the pilot wants to go. Likewise, the tongue is a small part of the body, but it makes great boasts. Consider what a great forest is set on fire by a small spark. The tongue also is a fire, a world of evil among the parts of the body. It corrupts the whole person, sets the whole course of his life on fire, and is itself set on fire by hell. All kinds of animals, birds, reptiles and creatures of the sea are being tamed and have been tamed by man, but no man can tame the tongue. It is a restless evil, full of deadly poison. With the tongue we praise our Lord and Father, and with it we curse men, who have been made in God's likeness.

Out of the same mouth come praise and cursing. My brothers, this should not be. Can both fresh water and saltwater flow from the same spring?"

And finally, these words that seem to wrap his total experience of dealing with dangerous words much like the words aimed at his brother Jesus:

"Brothers, do not slander one another. Anyone who speaks against his brother or judges him speaks against the law and judges it. When you judge the law, you are not keeping it, but sitting in judgment on it" (James 4:11).

These powerful expressions are spoken out of a deep understanding through encounter from both sides of the subject matter.

James grasped the depths of the literal fight to control the tongue and exactly where the destructive power comes from when he wrote,

"The tongue also is a fire, a world of evil among the parts of the body. It corrupts the whole person, sets the whole course of his life on fire, and is itself set on fire by hell" (James 3:6).

The powers of hell endeavored to use the words of Christ's own family in an effort to derail his mission given by the Heavenly Father on behalf of the whole world for all of time.

Who better to write about this subject than the very one who experienced, in an incredibly personal way, exactly how the sinless nature of Christ can change the human shortcomings of the depths of self-focus, pain creating unfettered levels of immaturity, and an unbridled tongue?

Here is perhaps the toughest issue within the family that Jesus desires us to learn and give place to in our own families: *We must learn to control our tongue, what we say, and how we say it, to all members of our family.*

I have often thought it interesting that one of the names for Jesus Christ the Messiah is, the "Word."

Yes, here is the aspect of his name that reflects what is so important in life—our words. Jesus lived out, in the sight and earshot of his family, those close to him, and all of mankind, as God with us—a living testimony of God inspired words. These are words of God's loving power and desire to dwell with us through Jesus, so we can visualize and hear in our hearts and minds the very nature of who God himself is.

How vastly important it is for us to understand as best we can that our words matter and are controlled, either in the heavenly love of God, or the dark agenda of evil. Does that sound overly dramatic to you? Well, ill-placed words can be just that, and bring deep hurt that can live on in another for years.

On the other hand, God blessed words can play a life-changing impactful role in someone's world for a lifetime.

Have you ever experienced a moment where you spoke in such harshness that you wondered where that came from? Now you know that unless you allow the Spirit of Christ to control your words, there will be times your words are used to destroy to a level you didn't really mean or can't believe you reached.

The manner in which Jesus spoke resurrecting life into those who lost theirs, spoke healing into sickness, and spoke in legitimate power of rebuke—calming the waves, or even removing demons of death and destruction—was a demonstration of the power and love of the words of heaven.

Jesus' very reputation through centuries of time is based upon the power of his words. Even to non-believers.

"And all spoke well of him and marveled at the gracious words that were coming from his mouth. And they said, 'Is not this Joseph's son?'" (Luke 4:22)

Throughout history, many non-believers, skeptics, and members of other faiths have acknowledged the profound impact of Jesus Christ's words, teachings, and personality, often expressing admiration for his moral and philosophical contributions. Here are a few notable kind words about Jesus from such perspectives:

1. **Mahatma Gandhi** - Although he did not embrace Christianity, Gandhi held Jesus in high esteem. He famously said, "I like your Christ. I do not like your Christians. Your Christians are so unlike your Christ." Gandhi admired Jesus' teachings on non-violence and compassion, considering the Sermon on the Mount a beautiful testament to the power of nonviolence and love.

2. **Albert Einstein** - The renowned physicist, although not adhering to orthodox Christianity, expressed his respect for Jesus as a historical figure. In an interview with the Saturday Evening Post in 1929, Einstein said, "As a child, I received instruction both in the Bible and in the Talmud. I am a Jew, but I am enthralled by the luminous figure of the Nazarene." He also stated, "No one can read the Gospels without feeling the actual presence of Jesus. His personality pulsates in every word. No myth is filled with such life."

3. **Napoleon Bonaparte** - Napoleon, known for his ambition and historical influence, reportedly had moments of reflection on spiritual matters, particularly about Jesus. He is quoted as saying, "Alexander, Caesar, Charlemagne, and I myself have founded empires; but upon what did these creations of our genius depend? Upon force. Jesus alone founded his empire upon love, and to this very day, millions would die for him."

4. **Friedrich Nietzsche** - Although Nietzsche is often remembered for his critical views on Christianity, calling it a "slave morality," he expressed a complex respect for Jesus. Nietzsche saw Jesus as the ultimate "free spirit" and admired his ability to stand apart from the societal norms of his

time. In "The Antichrist," Nietzsche wrote, "There was only one Christian, and he died on the cross."

These reflections, even from those who do not follow Christian faith, underscore a universal respect for Jesus' ethical words and unmatched presence.

We are not any different really. The words we use, and how we use them, establishes our own reputations and how others think of and talk about us both now and long after we are gone.

There is such amazing power in words.

Think about this astounding fact—it was with words that our entire world and universe was spoken into existence.

"By faith we understand that the universe was created by the *word* of God, so that what is seen was not made out of things that are visible" (Hebrews 11:3).

The very definition of the Big Bang theory is that something was made out of nothing in a moment where all that was needed for life came into existence within milliseconds of its materiality. How very biblical an explanation of creation without many scientists understanding they are corroborating the very essence and power of God and Scripture itself.

Arno Penzias, the Nobel Prize-winning scientist who co-discovered the cosmic microwave background radiation that provided strong support for the Big Bang in the first place, states:

"The best data we have are exactly what I would have predicted, had I nothing to go on but the five Books of Moses, the Psalms, the Bible as a whole."

Perhaps Penzias was thinking of the words of David in Psalm 8:3 that reads:

"When I consider your heavens, the work of your fingers, the moon and the stars, which you have set in place, what is man that you are mindful of him?"

Additionally, our words are forever on record.

We are coming to realize in our current mode of technology that our emails, texts, and tweets never disappear as they are saved on somebody's server somewhere. I wonder, if we will ever fully comprehend that even in the spiritual world this is also so. If we did, we would surely be more mindful and careful with our words?

Consider this Scripture from the words of Jesus:

"I tell you, on the day of judgment people will give account for every careless word they speak, for by your words you will be justified, and by your words you will be condemned" (Matthew 12:36-38).

All of us can think of examples of persons that can build up others with the way they speak and relate. And we can also think of far more individuals that have a venomous vocabulary that kills any constructive spirit of personal reinforcement in the room.

The Bible further advises us as to how we are to use our words:

"Let no corrupting talk come out of your mouths, but only such as is good for building up, as fits the occasion, that it may give grace to those who hear" (Ephesians 4:29).

Negative, damaging, destructive words can, and often do, destroy. And nowhere are we freer with our words than within the confines of our own family. Yet when these moments arise, controlling the tongue seems to be as excruciatingly difficult as it is important.

It is through our words that we bring a healing atmosphere to those lives that are dearest to us.

Is your home a haven of peace and escape from a world made of harsh and degrading words? Words not only bring peace to our homes but is also how we are saved for eternity.

I will leave you with one of the most important passages in all the Bible concerning the words that come from your mouth:

"… because, if you confess with your mouth that Jesus is Lord and believe in your heart that God raised him from the dead, you will be saved. For with the heart one believes and is justified, and with the mouth one confesses and is saved" (Romans 10:9 and 10).

You see, I told you your words are powerful!

Eternally powerful!

Chapter Nine

Forgiveness and the Family

"To love is something,

    To be loved is something more,

        But to love and be loved, that's everything."

            ~ Unknown

9

For years, I hosted and produced radio programming. In so doing, I had the opportunity to interview a number of well-known, even famous, people. One such person was Adolph Coors IV.

Addy, as they call him, was the heir of the Coors Brewery Company. When he was a teenager, his father stopped one morning on a narrow bridge on the way to work to help a man he thought to be stranded with car trouble. As it turned out, the man had set up the 44-year-old Coors patriarch after monitoring his every move for weeks. He kidnapped Adolph Coors III and eventually, after demanding a ransom of $500,000 with the promise to release Mr. Coors, killed Adolph Coors III in cold blood. The kidnapper never tried to obtain the ransom. He simply disappeared. Adolph Coors III's body would not be found for seven months.

I watched Addy as he told me that from that day forward, he had one goal in mind — to find the man who killed his father and kill him in pure unadulterated vengeance. That's what drove him! Everything he did moving forward was to prepare himself for the moment he would encounter this man. He took martial arts classes to learn the art of killing. He joined the Marines to become even more efficient at the art.

Then it happened. The police solved the crime and arrested the man guilty of the murder. His name was **Joe Corbitt**. The case went to court. Corbitt was found guilty and sentenced to life in prison.

But Addy still had a hole in his heart. As far as he was concerned, justice had not been served! The murderer was still alive.

Then, through a series of events, and a search for peace in his life, Addy found the Christ of forgiveness. He told me how Jesus not only changed his life but saved his soul. That is a ***story*** that was turned into a ***testimony*** because Addy overcame hatred and determined to offer Christ-like forgiveness in its place.

But there is more.

After a considerable amount of time had passed, Addy determined he needed to meet the man who took his father's life. He went to the prison where Joe Corbitt was housed and requested an audience. However, Corbitt refused. Multiple times Addy tried to see face to face the man who took the life of his father but each time, he was refused.

He went again on a weekend to make one last effort to meet with Joe Corbitt, but this time he took with him a Bible as a gift. Once again, Joe Corbitt refused to see Addy. So, Addy opened the inside cover of the Bible and wrote the following:

"Mr. Corbitt, I trust this Bible brings you comfort. I have come to visit you for the purpose of asking for your forgiveness. You see, in anger for what happened to my father, I have murdered you a thousand times in my mind. Please forgive me. God Bless you, Adolph Coors IV"

Sometime later, Addy joined a prison ministry that had been created by Chuck Colson called, Prison Fellowship International. As they went to minister to inmates one Saturday morning, Addy found himself heading into a prison he had been many times. They began with a meet and greet in the warden's office. As they were introducing themselves to the warden, it came time for Addy to introduce himself.

"So you're the son of Adolph Coors III?" the warden asked.

"Yes sir. That was my dad."

"I must say Mr. Coors, you have greatly impacted my prison. The day you came to see the man who murdered your father, and you left a Bible for him with a message inside, I want you to know that not only did that inmate receive the Bible, but that Bible has been passed throughout this prison. And the message you wrote inside has touched countless lives and changed this facility."

James discovered first-hand the loving patience and forgiveness offered him through the Lord's personal example of a perfectly consistent and controlled tongue, and the corresponding relationships that followed based on God's enduring love demonstrated by his own brother, Jesus.

Because of this, James could write with unequalled knowledge concerning this side of the human condition and God's faithfulness to forgive as he wrote in the simple accuracy and exactitude of the truth:

"If he has sinned, he will be forgiven" (James 5:15b).

All family members must know that when blunders happen, *and they will*, forgiveness will be offered, no matter how severe the blunder. This is not only what Jesus offers the world, but what he offered his family just as God offers that same forgiveness to us His children.

In the family concept of "tough love," we most often focus more on the "tough" part rather than on the "love" part.

The love of Christ, for us as a member of His family, is the most formidable and overcoming power the universe has ever known. And yes, it is even strong enough to change your family. Yet, in simultaneous fashion, this love is the most forgiving compassionate love the world has ever encountered.
Think for a moment of Jesus and his willingness to forgive. How would it impact your family should you be willing to offer a similar forgiving heart to those with whom you live? And if you dare think, even for a moment, as to whether your

forgiveness is deserved, let me remind you that the level of perfection many demand of others would leave even themselves disqualified a forgiving nod.

Consider this example of forgiveness and how it would impact your family? Remember the story of casting the first stone in John Chapter 8? Here it is:

"So when they continued asking Him, He raised Himself up and said to them, 'He who is without sin among you, let him throw a stone at her first.' And again, He stooped down and wrote on the ground.

Then those who heard *it,* being convicted by *their* conscience, went out one by one, beginning with the oldest *even* to the last. And Jesus was left alone, and the woman standing in the midst. When Jesus had raised Himself up and saw no one but the woman, He said to her, 'Woman, where are those accusers of yours? Has no one condemned you?'

She said, 'No one, Lord.'

And Jesus said to her, 'Neither do I condemn you; go and sin no more' "(John 8:6-11).

The Bible never made a case that the woman was wrongly accused and innocent. All we know is that the woman was *forgiven*.

Wow! Who of us in our own families are so perfect that we could ever cast a first stone—or throw the first blaming zinger—of any family issue at another?

In any personal squabble what would make one closer to another and build a lasting and trustworthy relationship? Being right? Or offering or receiving forgiveness. In any difficult circumstance, it is just as powerful, quite possibly even more so, to be forgiven or to offer forgiveness. Yet how often do we not choose this priceless remedy opting instead for the self-centered ego builder of thinking in total pretense that we are so extremely right?

One other thing I notice in this Scripture passage. Notice the moment that the accusers began to leave?

"Then those who heard *it,* being convicted by *their* conscience, went out one by one, beginning with the **oldest** *even* to the last" (John 8:9).

Isn't it interesting that the conviction of their consciences began with the *oldest?*

Was this a statement of a level of realization based upon maturity? I doubt it. I rather think it is based upon the fact that the older of the gathered became aware that their longevity simply meant they had more for which to be forgiven. This realization of truth must have landed powerfully upon them as it came directly from being in the presence of the person of Jesus the Christ himself. What an overwhelmingly powerful cacophony of silence had to have occurred as Jesus was personally shielding the life of this woman and not the self-proclaimed wise and self-righteous religious influencers of the day! Can you imagine?

This godly level of protection and forgiveness had to permeate through Jesus into his family. How do I know this? Because it was not just imparted to them in words, but it was lived out among and to them—and a member of Jesus' own family said so.

Here are the words of James:

"Whatever is good and perfect comes to us from God. He is the One Who made all light. He does not change. No shadow is made by His turning. He gave us our new lives through the truth of His Word only because He wanted to. We are the first children in His family" (James 1:17 and 18 - The Living Bible - TLB).

Do you see what James is testifying to here? He is speaking about the new life gifted to him, his family, and others around him—that all the good that came to their lives came to them through whom? Through "His" (God's) Word—Jesus. And he said something else of supreme importance here we cannot miss. Jesus did all of this, not because he somehow had to, but *"only because He wanted to."*

Again, the "Word" in James' letter is Jesus. John Chapter One made James' thoughts even clearer when it was written:

"In the beginning was the Word, and the Word was with God, and the Word was God (John 1:1).

The Word became *flesh* and *made his dwelling among us*. We have seen his glory, the glory of the one and only Son, who came from the Father, full of grace and truth" (John 1:14).

In the phrase written by James where he stated, "We are the first children in His family," James was essentially sharing with you and me that the goodness, the light of truth, the perfection of the love and forgiveness of Jesus, changed his family to the point that his earthly family had the honor of also being some of the very "first children" in this greater family of God.

How incredible! We know that the final outcome of Jesus' impact upon his own family was that he fulfilled his promise of John 6:39 when he declared:

"I shall lose none of all that he has given me ..."

When we forgive others, and experience forgiveness, something tender and wonderful happens in our hearts and within the four walls of our home. We experience the very presence of Christ himself who taught us what forgiveness truly is. Remember his willingness to forgive even those about to put him to death?

"And when they had come to the place called Calvary, there they crucified Him, and the criminals, one on the right hand and the other on the left. Then Jesus said, "Father, forgive them, for they do not know what they do." And they divided His garments and cast lots" (Luke 23:33-34 NKJV).

What strikes me most about this passage, demonstrating the boundless forgiveness of Jesus, is that he willingly forgave despite his knowing they were about to steal from him his last earthly possessions.

How shallow and undeserving they were — yet he forgave them. That is the true meaning of genuine forgiveness. In actuality, are we any better than they?

We don't have to qualify for his forgiveness. It has already been granted. Our only responsibility is to *accept* it.

The flip side is also true. Who are we to demand that someone else must somehow qualify for our forgiveness no matter how dastardly the action against us?

How would our relationships change, how would our family change, if that were the case between us and those with whom we are struggling?

Forgiveness is not a Scriptural suggestion. The Bible tells us it is something we "must do." And we must offer a forgiveness in the manner of Jesus. We forgive no matter the shallowness of those to whom we are offering.

There must *not* be a qualification to our forgiveness of another. We are to forgive in this manner for the benefit of all involved, including—and maybe especially—ourselves.

When we do not obey the word of the Lord we will always be lacking in our spiritual lives and all that we endeavor to accomplish relationally and in life at large, as God's blessings will not be fully realized outside of obedience. Offer and receive forgiveness and blessing so you may live a fulfilled life in Christ.

"But when you are praying, first forgive anyone you are holding a grudge against, so that your Father in heaven will forgive your sins, too." Mark 11:25 NLT

Is this power of Christ's love and forgiveness the basis of your family relationships?

What must your family do to truly learn from Christ's earthly family that will make the relationships within your household that for which other families will wish for and desire to emulate?

The truthful answer to the question is this:
In order to offer and experience this level of empowered love in relationships, Jesus and His Spirit of love and forgiveness, must live in the midst of your family and home.

His presence, His attitude, His words, changes everything.

Chapter Ten

Respect and the Family

10

"The bond that links your true family is not one of blood,
but of respect and joy in each other's life."
Richard Bach

Sir Nicholas Winton's act of immense courage and respect for human life offers a powerful example of how respect and empathy can transcend boundaries and change destinies. In 1938, as Europe edged closer to World War II, Nicholas Winton, a young British stockbroker, planned to spend his holiday skiing in Switzerland. However, a friend convinced him to visit Prague, Czechoslovakia, instead, to help with refugee welfare work.

Upon arriving in Prague, Winton was moved by the plight of Jewish children at risk from the impending Nazi invasion. Recognizing the urgency of the situation, he took it upon himself to organize an operation that would come to be known as the Czech Kindertransport. Winton set up an office in a hotel in Prague and started collecting the names and details of children who needed to escape. He worked tirelessly to find foster homes for these children in Britain and arranged for their safe passage across Europe.

Winton faced immense challenges, including bureaucratic hurdles in multiple countries and the need to raise enough money to fund the transports. He also had to persuade the British government to allow the entry of the refugee children. His respect for each child's life drove him to forge British government documents when official permissions stalled.

In total, Nicholas Winton managed to arrange for 669 children to be transported to Britain, saving them from the concentration camps and certain death. The last train, which was scheduled to leave on September 1, 1939, was prevented from departing by the outbreak of World War II; sadly, none of the 250 children scheduled to leave on that train were seen again.

Winton's remarkable efforts remained largely unknown for over 50 years until 1988, when his wife found a detailed scrapbook in their attic. The scrapbook contained lists of the children, including their parents' names and the names and addresses of the families that took them in. This discovery eventually led to a moving episode on the BBC television program "That's Life!" where Winton was reunited with dozens of the children he had saved.

Sir Nicholas Winton's story is not just a tale of rescue and survival; it is a profound lesson in respect and human decency. He saw the intrinsic value of each life he saved, treating every child with the utmost respect, regardless of their background. His actions remind us that respect can manifest as profound acts of bravery and compassion, capable of altering the course of history. His legacy teaches us that one person's respect and care for others can indeed save lives and create a ripple effect across generations.

In the family, there is nothing more important than appropriate respect for those living with you, and more importantly, in authority over you. Many arguments immediately bubble up as to why this can't *always* be the case. The "what ifs" of life begin to surface. And many times, the general reasoning can make total sense as to why a parent or older family member simply cannot be revered.

However, understand that I am not making a case for us to "revere" all *persons* in authority over us. I am, however, calling upon us to "appropriately respect" the position they hold, or held, within the family.

Give my reasoning a chance here.

It is important to understand that in specific and difficult cases—such as examples of abuse and other kinds of indecent, and often unimaginably illicit behaviors—it is impossible to esteem that person.
There are ways, nonetheless, to honor the *position* (even a parental position) that an individual holds, or held, in our lives while not admiring their weak, even dark, behavior.

There is a place of respect that is important for that specific position in life we cannot loose. And we must hold tightly to our general respect for that place and position as we live out our lives. And it is an important issue in dealing with respect for positions of life for others too, especially our children.

It is important for us, therefore, to redefine—for the generation to follow—how to aptly view specific stations of authority. In other words, it is important for us to help to reestablish a proper respect for that position as we live out new roles in the reflection of Jesus.

It is important too, for all involved, to understand how God outlined that particular role. That will be accomplished through examples shared with us in Scripture, in being a life example we live out through our own lives, as well as through persons God dramatically places in our lives.

I have found that God has a brilliant way of placing true to life examples in our path through the years, to redefine life roles, that need to be seen in a different light as we need them redeemed and reidentified, so the family can move forward.

This is precisely why it is important to spend time where we often will find such people. People that can be a "father figure" to us where we did not have a fitting one prior. The same is true of a "mother figure," or sibling, or any family member for that matter, we missed out on in certain stages of our lives.

How often have you heard someone say that a particular friend was "closer than family," or like a brother or sister, or an aunt or uncle? This is to what I am referring.

We may find them in the church, or through healthy godly friendships or relationships at work. Or we may even find them as our neighbors, or other acquaintances that move in and out of our lives through the years. They may come from a variety of points in life. But if we are striving for growth in our lives, and we are allowing God to lead this growth, they will come and a vacated role of needed respect and authority in our lives will be filled.

Then, there are simply moments in life where we find ourselves in a place of disagreement with that special loved one—that trusted person in authority over us. It is especially in these circumstances that we very much need to be careful with our responses, both to them and in-front of others. Let me give you a prime example from the family of Jesus.

Jesus clearly was fulfilling a purposefully placed strategy through coming to this earth as Immanuel—"God with us" (Isaiah 7:14, Matthew 1:23)—to introduce himself to the world and finally fulfill his prophetic role as Messiah and Savior. There were times, as we have discussed, that his family simply did not understand the overlap of his role as family member and son within the family itself, and his role as Savior of the World given him by his Father in Heaven.

So, how exactly did Jesus respond in such circumstances? Let's take a look and see. In John 2:1-11 we have just such an example:

"On the third day a wedding took place at Cana in Galilee. Jesus' mother was there, and Jesus and his disciples had also been invited to the wedding. When the wine was gone, Jesus' mother said to him, 'They have no more wine.'

'Woman, why do you involve me?' Jesus replied. 'My hour has not yet come.'
His mother said to the servants, 'Do whatever he tells you.'
Nearby stood six stone water jars, the kind used by the Jews for ceremonial washing, each holding from twenty to thirty gallons.
Jesus said to the servants, 'Fill the jars with water'; so they filled them to the brim.
Then he told them, 'Now draw some out and take it to the master of the banquet.'
They did so, and the master of the banquet tasted the water that had been turned into wine. He did not realize where it had come from, though the servants who had drawn the water knew. Then he called the bridegroom aside and said, 'Everyone brings out the choice wine first and then the cheaper wine after the guests have had too much to drink; but you have saved the best till now.'

What Jesus did here in Cana of Galilee was the *first* of the signs through which he revealed his glory; and his disciples believed in him."

The first thing that must be recognized here is that Jesus' mother, Mary, knew that Jesus had the ability to take care of this situation—somehow. She may not have known what exactly he was going to do to fix this embarrassing problem, but she knew he had the ability to do it.

She also knew he was *not* going to deal with this issue. She seemed to understand Jesus had a particular timeline by which he was operating and most likely, saving a red-faced groom from massive embarrassment was not going to be a trigger point for the hand of God to move.

So, for whatever reason, that we will never know, Mary took charge of the moment.

Jesus was clearly annoyed. His response did not begin with some warm refrain as in, "oh mom" or "mother." It was a rather stern sounding, "woman."

I can't say that I never dared call my mom, "woman," as I write this with a nervous smile. No, Jesus referred to her in a term the original Greek used as, "*gynē*."

This specific word has a very universal meaning and reference that would be used toward any woman, including a stranger. The use of that word for his mother demonstrated clearly, he was not pleased at all with the position she placed him in lest you think I am taking some poetic license in my scriptural interpretation.

His annoyance was even more clearly evidenced in what he said to her as he implied that she knew exactly what she was doing in her actions leading us to wonder ourselves why she did such a thing. Jesus was clearly miffed as to her choices here as he said,

"Woman, why do you involve me? My hour has not yet come."

Yet, what did he do versus all the things he could have done to demonstrate his displeasure?

In spite of the uncomfortable situation he now found himself in, (lovingly created by his mother), Jesus still showed respect for her position by ultimately doing as she had asked of him—performing what is often referred to as his first Messianic miracle as the Bible states:

"What Jesus did here in Cana of Galilee was the *first* of the signs through which he revealed his glory."

Think about this for a moment. Jesus could have really let her have it good with some serious God-like rebuke stating how little she understood the importance of who he is and what he was about to do for the world. He could have raised his voice and let his feelings be unmistakably known (throwing in a little lightning and thunderclap for effect) making his point even clearer.

And he could have done it in such a manner that, for sure, the story would have found its way into somebody's New Testament chapter, so humanity could see for all time how "God with us" put Mary in her place. After all, he is God you know.

But no. He had utmost respect for her. He respected her feelings and her position in life as his mother. He also respected his own role as her son too.

So often we forget, that when we show disrespect for another, we are showing the same amount of disrespect for ourselves. Conversely, the opposite can be said as Jesus himself taught after this episode with his mother in Matthew 7 verse 12:

"So in everything, do to others what you would have them do to you, for this sums up the Law and the Prophets."

I really like the way this Scripture reads in the New American Standard Bible:

"In everything, therefore, treat people the same way you want them to treat you, for this is the Law and the Prophets."

Jesus didn't just talk a good game. He lived it out as the true and only sinless vessel to ever have walked this earth.

Think of what that means!

He was not only sinless in his words—he was also sinless in his actions and responses. He was sinless in all his thoughts and his mind. And he fully demonstrated this as he was honest in the fact that he was annoyed, yet he did not go over the line with an angry arrogant verbal display.

Consider this Scripture as to the sinless nature of Jesus:

"For we do not have a high priest who is unable to empathize with our weaknesses, but we have one who has been tempted in every way, just as we are—yet he did not sin" (Hebrews 4:15).

Or this Scripture concerning the same point:

"God made him who had no sin to be sin for us, so that in him we might become the righteousness of God (II Corinthians 5:21).

And then, these weighty words from Jesus that will impact us on so many levels of our lives should we choose to be obedient to God:

"You are the salt of the earth. But if the salt loses its saltiness, how can it be made salty again? It is no longer good for anything, except to be thrown out and trampled underfoot. You are the light of the world. A town built on a hill cannot be hidden. Neither do people light a lamp and put it under a bowl. Instead they put it on its stand, and it gives light to everyone in the house. In the same way, let your light shine before others, that they may see your good deeds and glorify your Father in heaven" (Matthew 5:13-16).

Jesus was speaking to us, absolutely! But it is as though he was reminding himself of this incredible role he was playing in order to save the world, including our families.

Remember, Jesus referred to himself as, "The Light of the world." He wasn't about to preach at us words from his Heavenly Father that were not good for him as well. That is the humility only He could live out not clinging to His rights as God.

Consider this Scripture from Philippians 2:5-8:

[5] In your relationships with one another, have the same mindset as Christ Jesus:

[6] Who, being in very nature God,
   did not consider equality with God something to be used to his own advantage;
[7] rather, he made himself nothing
   by taking the very nature of a servant,
   being made in human likeness.
[8] And being found in appearance as a man,
   he humbled himself

> by becoming obedient to death—
> > even death on a cross!

It was in the example of His light, and not in name only, that darkness was destroyed.

"When Jesus spoke again to the people, he said, "I am the light of the world. Whoever follows me will never walk in darkness but will have the light of life" (John 8:12).

And ...

"While I am in the world, I am the light of the world" (John 9:5).

Now, looking back at Matthew 5, exchange the word "earth" with the word "family," and see now how it reads:

"You are the salt of the *family*. But if the salt loses its saltiness, how can it be made salty again? It is no longer good for anything, except to be thrown out and trampled underfoot. You are the light of the *family*. A town built on a hill cannot be hidden. Neither do people light a lamp and put it under a bowl. Instead they put it on its stand, and it gives light to everyone in the house. In the same way, let your light shine before others (in your family), that they may see your good deeds and glorify your Father in heaven."

Oh, to strive for the family ambiance, setting, environment, mood, tone we could live in if we were only able to grasp a small portion of the example of Christ—that even our failures would not be met with deceit to get even. Or that we would not return insults for the insults thrown at us. Or that the concept of retaliation simply exists no more because anger is squashed into oblivion by true Godly love and forgiveness!

That our conflicts, produced in darkness, would become testimonies of Son-lit victory as we overcame the darkness by reflecting the Light of the World, Jesus, upon them. Wow! How wonderful would that be.

And it is not just a good idea for us to try. Scripture says that in knowing Jesus, we are called to this kind of living. It becomes a truth that cannot be ignored as we have now been exposed to this life example of Christ himself—desired for us by God our Father.

Consider this Scripture:

"To this you were called, because Christ suffered for you, leaving you an example, that you should follow in his steps. 'He committed no sin, and no deceit was found in his mouth' (Isaiah 53:9).

When they hurled their insults at him, he did not retaliate; when he suffered, he made no threats. Instead, he entrusted himself to him who judges justly" (I Peter 2:21-23).

Oh, how we and our families must and need to learn from this example of pure unadulterated love Jesus had for his mother, and all the members of his family.

Then, this indescribable love and respect Jesus had for his mother was shown us again in one of the most wrenchingly difficult moments Jesus faced in his time on this earth.

"Near the cross of Jesus stood his mother, his mother's sister, Mary the wife of Clopas, and Mary Magdalene. When Jesus saw his mother there, and the disciple whom he loved standing nearby, he said to her, 'Woman, here is your son,' and to the disciple, 'Here is your mother.' From that time on, this disciple took her into his home" (John 19:25-27).
Notice the line in this Scripture, "'Woman, here is your son,' and to the disciple, 'Here is your mother.'" The use of the term "woman" from the first miracle of Jesus in John 2:4, as he turned water into wine, is the exact same word we see used in the original Greek in this verse in John 19:26, "*gynē.*"

The spirit of the moment between the two passages is so completely different, yet, Jesus is again saying to her, "woman," not mom or mother. But the reason now seems to be that he has removed himself as her earthly son and replaced his physical presence with the disciple whom he (Jesus) loved.

He knew he could never physically be her son ever again, so he removed himself from the role to fully define, for them both, who was now responsible for her on this earth. What amazing humility for a first-born son to relinquish that position for the sake of his mother. Relating as a first-born son myself, there is amazing depths of feeling as this needed redefining played out. For Jesus gave up his mantle as first-born son, and his place in the Godhead, to become a willing sacrifice for all of us and our homes. What an emotionally grueling moment to endure.

And that disciple effectively, from that moment on, took her to his home and cared for her.

Jesus is demonstrating to us that no matter the circumstances we find ourselves, no matter how dire they may be, true love is always aware of the needs of those we love.

Jesus was making sure his mother was going to be cared for even at the moment of his dying breath. That is a love that cannot be found outside the purity of heart only gifted to us from the very Being of God. We just do not have it naturally within ourselves.

There is never a time where it is acceptable to throw out all that is Godly love for a self-serving moment. It just doesn't fit—ever. When God's love fully washes over us, we cannot move in and out of this uniquely powerful, yet immeasurably compassionate love. It fully engulfs us in all our moments.

This is how we are changed. This is how our family is truly changed. This is how true respect is captured within the family unit.

No matter how difficult the moment, God's love wins out.

It is God's love, in the Spirit of Christ that, when it is experienced in all its fullness, changes lives, homes, and the world.

And should we step out of the salt and light that brings all good taste to life and makes truth easier to see, it becomes such a foreign moment for us that we can never dwell there.

This is the power that will change us, and our families, forever!

Chapter Eleven

Held Together by Him

"It would be very difficult to explain why the universe should have begun in just this way, except as the act of a God who intended to create beings like us."
Steven Hawking, A Brief History of Time

11

Francis Collins, an acclaimed geneticist, and the former director of the National Institutes of Health (NIH) is renowned for his leadership of the Human Genome

Project, which successfully mapped the human DNA structure. His journey from atheism to Christianity is a compelling narrative about how scientific inquiry and profound personal experiences can lead to spiritual belief.

Born in 1950, Collins was raised in a family of little religious inclination and considered himself an atheist by the time he was a graduate student in physical chemistry at Yale University. His transition from atheism began during his time in medical school at the University of North Carolina at Chapel Hill, where he encountered patients facing terminal illnesses. The strength and serenity with which they faced death, rooted in their faith, challenged his atheistic views, and sparked his curiosity about the nature of belief.

Collins decided to explore the basis of religious faith intellectually, initially to challenge it. He read widely about various world religions and philosophical systems, but it was C.S. Lewis' book, "Mere Christianity," that particularly struck a chord. Lewis' argument that moral law suggests a moral lawgiver prompted Collins to reconsider the existence of God. Over time, he found himself convinced not only of God's existence but of the Christian narrative as the most compelling explanation of human existence and the basis for his experiences.

His conversion to Christianity did not come at the expense of his scientific work; instead, it enriched his understanding of the universe. Collins has since been a vocal advocate for the compatibility of science and faith, arguing that belief in God can coexist with a commitment to scientific inquiry.

He has written about his experiences and views in the book "The Language of God: A Scientist Presents Evidence for Belief," which outlines how he reconciles his faith with his work in genetics.

Collins' story is particularly significant because it illustrates that the pursuit of scientific knowledge can coexist with, and even complement, a deep personal faith. His professional achievements and personal journey reflect his belief in a rational universe underpinned by divine creation, showing that the realms of science and religion, often seen as conflicting, can indeed be integrated harmoniously in one's worldview.

Francis Collins continues to be a leading voice in discussions about the ethical implications of scientific advances and the importance of faith in a technological world. His life is a testament to the possibility of a profound and respectful dialogue between faith and science.

Many of you reading this are doing your very best to hold your family together. I want you to recognize the incredible power waiting for you to tap into. Consider this remarkable Scripture:

"The Son is the image of the invisible God, the firstborn over all creation. For in him all things were created: things in heaven and on earth, visible and invisible, whether thrones or powers or rulers or authorities; all things have been created through him and for him. He is before all things, and in him all things hold together" (Colossians 1:15-17).

He, Jesus, is the firstborn of literally everything! He of course was the first born of his earthly family, and He is the first-born over all creation, the greatest family of all. All things were through and for Him — Jesus. The list is remarkable!

Did you see what was included in that list? All things in heaven and on earth, visible and invisible, whether thrones or powers or rulers or authorities; all things have been created through him and for him.

What truly resonates with me is the idea that in Him, everything in this universe is held together—absolutely everything! That encompasses your family and your household as well.

May I just say that I believe we most often underestimate who Jesus really is. Read this passage as a resume, a resounding statement of powerful fact, and realize, if He can hold all things together — All Things — he can hold whatever is happening in your and my life and family together.

Have you heard of the scientific concept of the Fine Tuner? The first time I heard mention of this terminology was on a radio interview with Stephen Hawking's closest collaborator of the theory he put forward in his book, *A Brief History of Time*.

Hawking spent years in effort to prove that our universe was not the only one existing that could sustain life. He came up with his "multiverse" theory that essentially stated that there had to be millions of universes similar to our own; that our universe was not unique, therefore, a hypothetical collection of potentially diverse observable universes existed which would comprise everything needed to sustain life.

Let me say it again. JESUS is the FINE TUNER of the universe!

"The Son is the radiance of God's glory and the exact representation of his being, sustaining all things by his powerful word." Hebrews 1:3a NIV

Over the past 40 years, scientists have discovered a surprising fact about our universe: Against incredible odds, the numbers in basic physics are exactly as they need to be to accommodate the possibility and the sustainability of life.

If gravity had been slightly weaker, stars would not have exploded into supernovae, a crucial source of many of the heavier elements involved in life. Conversely, if gravity had been slightly stronger, stars would have lived for thousands rather than billions of years, not leaving enough time for biological evolution to take place. This is just one example – there are many others – of the "fine-tuning" of the laws of physics needed for the initial existence of life and the continual sustaining of life.

Some scientists and philosophers think the fine-tuning (the ongoing maintenance of this delicate balance for the existence of our universe and world as we know it) is powerful evidence for the existence of God. However, in his 2010 book The Grand Design (co-authored with Leonard Mlodinow), Stephen Hawking defended a naturalistic explanation of fine-tuning in terms of the multiverse hypothesis.

Hawking could not admit that the God of all creation got it right the first time.

After Hawking's death, many still hold out hope for a scientific account of fine-tuning. However, by ruling out one of the two scientifically credible options for doing this, Hawking and his partner in science, Thomas Hertog, have unwittingly strengthened the alternative explanation in terms of the existence of God.

Isn't it ironic that the atheist Stephen Hawking should, in his final contribution to science, make God's existence more probable to the community of science?

However, as long as the "fine-tuning" question remains open, the idea remains, and is only growing stronger, that the laws of the universe show that it must have been designed, and the designing inspired, conducted, and maintained by an intelligent creator.

As one of Hawking's co-authors and cohorts in science, Hertog commented regarding the fact that scientific evidence continues to prove the concept of Hawking's multiverse hypothesis to be less and less plausible said, "Stephen would say that, theoretically, it's almost like the universe had to be like this".

The Bible placed the entire answer of the creation of the world before us, and how Jesus came to our world choosing to become a member of a family when it was written in John Chapter 1:1-14

1 In the beginning was the Word, and the Word was with God, and the Word was God. **2** He was with God in the beginning. **3** Through him all things were made; without him nothing was made that has been made. **4** In him was life, and that life was the light of all mankind. **5** The light shines in the darkness, and the darkness has not overcome[a] it. **6** There was a man sent from God whose name was John. **7** He came as a witness to testify concerning that light, so that through him all might believe. **8** He himself was not the light; he came only as a witness to the light. **9** The true light that gives light to everyone was coming into the world. **10** He was in the world, and though the world was made through him, the world did not recognize him. **11** He came to that which was his own, but his own did not receive him. **12** Yet to all who did receive him, to those who believed in his name, he gave the right to become children of God— **13** children born not of natural descent, nor of human decision or a husband's will, but born of God. **14** The Word became flesh and made his dwelling among us. We have seen his glory, the glory of the one and only Son, who came from the Father, full of grace and truth.

This is the power you have in support behind you and the intentional design of your family! Think of that!

Fred Hoyle, the astronomer who coined the term "big bang," said that his atheism was "greatly shaken" by the continual unfolding of information.

One of the world's most renowned theoretical physicists, Paul Davies, has said that "the appearance of design is overwhelming."

Even the late atheist Christopher Hitchens agreed that "without question the fine-tuning argument was the most powerful argument of the other side."

Oxford University professor of Mathematics Dr. John Lennox has said, "The more we get to know about our universe, the more the hypothesis that there is a Creator . . . gains in credibility as the best explanation of why we are here."

We can never forget that history and science will only confirm that in the end—no matter who makes the argument, Creator God will always have the last and final word about all that transpires in the world and in your family.

Theoretical physicist and Anglican priest John Polkinghorne has stated: "Anthropic fine tuning is too remarkable to be dismissed as just a happy accident."

In 1961, physicist Robert H. Dicke claimed that certain forces in physics, such as gravity and electromagnetism, must be perfectly fine-tuned for life to exist in the universe.

Fred Hoyle also argued for a fine-tuned universe in his 1984 book *The Intelligent Universe*. "The list of anthropic properties, apparent accidents of a non-biological nature without which carbon-based and hence human life could not exist, is large and impressive", Hoyle wrote.

Belief in the fine-tuned universe led to the expectation that the Large Hadron Collider (LHC) would produce evidence of physics beyond the Standard Model, such as supersymmetry, but by 2012 results from the LHC had not produced evidence for supersymmetry at the energy scales it was able to probe.

I close with these thoughts reminding you of the power behind you, your family, and the ability for your trust and obedience to Jesus will fine tune your life and home just as he has held things together as the Fine Tuner of the universe. Here now is a quote from the writings of the Rev. Billy Graham:

"We must have faith in God the Creator, not in education or experience. The Bible begins with the simple words: 'In the beginning God….' These four words are the cornerstone of all existence and of all human history. Without God there could have been no beginning and no continuing. God was the creating power. By divine fiat, He brought form out of shapelessness, order out of disorder, and light out of darkness. If we try to rationalize God, we will fail. There are mysteries about God that we will never understand in this life. We should not think it strange that it is impossible to comprehend God intellectually, when it is equally impossible to explain many mysteries in the realm of matter. Who can fathom the law of gravity? Newton discovered it, but he could not explain it.

There are many arguments we could marshal to give evidence of the existence of God. We see objects that have no intellect, such as stars and planets, moving in a consistent pattern, cooperating with one another. Hence, it is evident that they achieve their movements not by accident but by design. If God can be fully proved by the human mind, then He is no greater than the mind that proves Him. Cry out to God, 'Lord… help my unbelief!'"

Again, I will say it. Whatever the challenge you are facing today, realize who it is standing in your corner with you. He is Jesus. God with us.

Remember—For in him all things were created: things in heaven and on earth, visible and invisible, whether thrones or powers or rulers or authorities; all things have been created through him and for him.

Do not underestimate who Jesus is, His power, His ability to hold All things together, or the depths of His love for you.

Give that challenge, that issue, that thing — ALL THINGS — to Him, and trust Jesus for the very best outcome because of His love for you and your family.

Chapter Twelve

Perfection in Motion

"I will behave wisely in a perfect way . . .
I will walk within my house with a perfect heart."
Psalm 101:2

12

In a quiet suburban neighborhood lived a little boy named Oliver, whose world revolved around his father, Jack. To Ollie, his dad was more than just a parent; he was a superhero without a cape, perfect in every way imaginable.

Jack was a firefighter, and his tales of bravery and heroism filled Ollie's young mind with awe and admiration. Every evening, Ollie would wait by the window, watching for his father's truck to pull into the driveway. As soon as Jack walked through the door, Oliver would run to him, eager to hear stories of the day's rescues. Whether it was saving a cat stuck in a tree or battling a fierce blaze to protect people's homes, Jack's stories captivated Ollie, who hung on to every word.

What made Jack perfect in Ollie's eyes wasn't just his bravery; it was also the small moments they shared. Every Saturday morning, they would go on adventures in the local park, sometimes pretending to be explorers discovering new lands, other times astronomers searching for distant stars. Jack taught Ollie how to ride a bike, cheering the loudest when he finally rode without training wheels.

One day, the local school organized a "Career Day," and Jack was invited to speak about his job. Oliver was bursting with pride as he introduced his father to his classmates. Jack arrived in his firefighter uniform, his badge shining. He spoke about fire safety and the importance of helping others, captivating the children with his charisma and kindness. To Ollie, this day was definitive proof that his dad was the greatest hero anyone could ever have.

However, the true test of Jack's perfection came one stormy night when a distress call pulled him away to a dangerous fire. The next morning, Ollie heard the news that there had been an accident. Fear gripped his heart as he waited for news about his father. Hours later, Jack returned home, limping badly but safe. He had saved two children from a burning house but had suffered personal injury.

That evening, as Jack rested on the couch, Ollie approached him quietly. He climbed up next to his father, took his hand, and said, "Daddy, you really are perfect. You save people, and you saved yourself because you came back to me." Tears welled up in Jack's eyes as he hugged Ollie tightly, realizing that his son's idea of perfection wasn't about being invincible; it was about being loving, brave, and most importantly, coming back home.

This story of Ollie and his father illustrates the profound admiration a child can have for a parent. Ollie's belief in his father's perfection was based not on Jack being flawless, but on his everyday acts of courage, love, and the undying commitment to his family and community. Through Oliver's eyes, Jack was perfect because he embodied the qualities of a true hero: bravery, love, and resilience.

Jesus is the perfect example of being nothing short of the very best of what family is supposed to offer. He didn't just come to our world boasting he was perfect. But rather, he demonstrated how to live in a manner that simply and precisely was the plan of the Father for a member of any family.

Jesus *is* perfection in motion.

Why did he feel the necessity of living out his brand of perfection in our midst? I mean, who are we that the creator of the universe would ever want to impress upon us such indescribable accomplishment as his boundless perfection in human form that only the Master of all in existence could deliver?
Simply put, we can't comprehend perfection in the realm of the Godhead. So why would he even try to make the effort?
Because He understood the importance being a living example really is. And He transferred all the importance of being that example into the family setting.

And to bringing it down to the simplest thought, those of us who are parents want our children to be proud of us … don't we?

Could it be that he simply loved us made in his image so much that he wanted and desired to actually live among us and personally show us the path to living well-rounded fulfilled lives where it really counts—in our own homes?

After all, we want what is the absolute best for our children don't we? Why would it not be the same for the Father of all things?

Just think what we could be if we were only a portion of what his hopes and dreams for us are!

We saw it earlier when James said:

"He gave us our new lives through the truth of His Word only because He wanted to" (James 1:18).

Break that sentence down and see what a great gift we have.

"He gave us our new lives" — He knew he was bringing worthwhile change to our existence that would remake us, as well as those around us,

"Through the truth" — What Jesus was demonstrating to us about family living was completely and fully trustworthy, so we need have no doubt in its ability to change our homes and lives for the better in and through that truth,

"Because he wanted to" — He chose to be with us, not because He had to! He already regarded us as family and wanted to be with us!

Did he live his life in front of all humanity so as to brazenly remind us of our shortcomings and our ineptitudes? No, of course not! He lived out his perfection in front of us to show us *we matter*!

He involved himself in our lives to make us the best we could be — for each other!

He lived a flawless life to give us a target for our own living!

He placed His son of perfection into our midst so we would ultimately be safe!

When Jesus said in Matthew 5:48, "Be perfect, therefore, as your heavenly Father is perfect," he wasn't sending us on an impossible mission. He was telling us to strive toward perfection, so we could have something to measure ourselves by. He told us to strive for perfection, so we could clearly recognize how we could do better each time we fell short, not so we would become judged and discouraged.

As we are growing up, we determine how to be a man or woman by measuring ourselves through what we see in mom and dad—do we not? After all, in a "perfect world," isn't that what parents are to do for their children? Parents are our example and teach us about life so we can accomplish more than the generation before us?

Isn't that the underlying value of having even older siblings? Isn't that the point of having a mentor? Isn't it all about growth and being better in life through our growing?

The Holy Trinity of Father, Son and Holy Spirit, is telling us that the three in one is willing to be so personally involved in our lives, that he—God himself—is willing to play the role of parent (Father), sibling (Son), and mentor (Holy Spirit) through the living example of the life of Jesus Christ on this earth, bringing God's love to us, and introducing us to the wisdom and comfort of the Holy Spirit. This is accomplished through all we are able to learn about his family, his personal relationships, and ministry.

He lived out his life in such a manner that we could visibly, not only see that something *could* be done better, but more importantly, how to *make* that something better. The "something" could be a response to a moment in life or our day-to-day living. It could have to do with a point of integrity in action, or even our being taught to tell the truth in difficult circumstances.

Whatever the "somethings" in life are, we learn how to deal with them through the prism of living with our family. Jesus came into his earthly family, so we could know how to deal with life by means of his God-centered perspective.

We all need competent loving examples for living. And there is no greater competence and trustworthy love than what is given us through Jesus Christ.

It simply comes down to this—God the Father cared so much about giving us a quality future of living, that he gave to us a road map for our lives through the sending of his only Son. He became our atonement for our sins bringing eternal safety for our souls, yes! But he also became our model to live by until the day comes that we make our way into eternity, to our heavenly home.

If we emulate the life of Jesus within the framework of our families, what are the key points of his endless perfection that we want to take from his life to plug into the pattern of our own family living? Three points come to mind.

Live in Selflessness

Jesus defined his personal mission simply when he said,

"For even the Son of Man did not come to be served, but to serve, and to give his life as a ransom for many" (Mark 10:45).

Think how your family would be different if the members of your family took this proclamation as their personal mission statement? I wonder how different our home and individual world would be if our spirit of self was lived through the perspective that Jesus defined for us in his own mission statement?

He did not come to be served but to serve … and to give his life.

Think of all we would be missing? Some old human traditions such as gossip, backbiting, selfish personal agendas, division, resentment, and even hatred. Would you be willing to give up those gems in exchange for the spirit of giving, forgiving, trust, servanthood and sacrifice? Kind of a no-brainer isn't it?!

How much would change at family gatherings and holidays if these attributes of Jesus became our family norm?

The next and obvious question then becomes, how could such a major miraculous transition occur in my family?

Well, I will at least tell you how the process begins.

It begins through personal example during a most difficult moment of family life. It will begin by the gifting of grace to someone that, by definitions of this world, did not deserve anything short of judgment.

It is in a moment like this that grace offered, anchored in massive love, can only be seen as coming from outside everything that is a norm for our world. That gift of grace will be recognized by all who witness it as having a uniquely holy and Godly quality beyond anything we would have to offer solely from ourselves.

For a scriptural example of this, within the framework of the family, I often return to the story of the prodigal son who requested his inheritance early, left the family, and lived his life for an extended period of time in a very reckless and risqué style.

Suddenly, he is in the position of being out of money and unable to take care of himself. This is where we pick up the story as told by Jesus in Scripture:

"When he came to his senses, he said, 'How many of my father's hired servants have food to spare, and here I am starving to death! I will set out and go back to my father and say to him: Father, I have sinned against heaven and against you. I am no longer worthy to be called your son; make me like one of your hired servants.' So he got up and went to his father.

But while he was still a long way off, his father saw him and was filled with compassion for him; he ran to his son, threw his arms around him and kissed him.

The son said to him, 'Father, I have sinned against heaven and against you. I am no longer worthy to be called your son.'

But the father said to his servants, 'Quick! Bring the best robe and put it on him. Put a ring on his finger and sandals on his feet. Bring the fattened calf and kill it. Let's have a feast and celebrate. For this son of mine was dead and is alive again; he was lost and is found.'" (Luke 15:17-24).

Forgiveness and change in our families begin when someone is willing to offer selfless sacrificial love, especially when the one offering that love is the one that has been wronged. The goodness of the Lord is recognized by all in such moments as this!

It is here that it is clearly seen that something just happened that is beyond anything we can generate in and of ourselves. Something has been gifted us through the loving touch of God.

The question we must answer if we really desire such a family moment like this is, "Am I willing to be the one who is the catalyst of change for my family? What price am I willing to pay for the priceless peace, love and breakthrough our family needs, to be all God intended us to be together?"

The example of Jesus coming to serve *is* the change agent that will cause all in your house to stop and wonder—what has just happened?

The answer?

Jesus has happened.

Live Without Judgment

One of the greatest challenges of family is found in overcoming the harshness of judgment. At times, we are so willing to believe the worst of family members that all that remains to us in our home is the residue of mistrust, jealousy and anger. What is sad about many of these circumstances is that most often they begin in misunderstanding due to the fact that someone jumped to a conclusion about another that was simply incorrect. We chose to believe the wrong conclusion — and ran with it.

Consider this central verse stating the supreme purpose of Jesus coming into our world:

"For God did not send his Son into the world to condemn the world, but to save the world through him" (John 3:17).

Now, for just a moment, insert the word "family" in place of the word "world" and see how that reads:

"For God did not send his Son into the *family* to condemn the *family*, but to save the *family* through him."

First of all, that works, because our family *is* our world. It is the central point of our existence.

And secondly, it works because it is just as truthful as the original text of John 3:17.

The breakdown of the family today is nothing short of a continuance of the heritage of the breakdown on this earth when disobedience and sin entered the door of that very first family home in the Garden of Eden.

It didn't take long for the massive breakdown to lead to the very first ever murder, and all that comes with such a dastardly crime such as lying, cover-up, and the eventual destruction of lives through the sentences of justice. Look how this heritage of murder has carried through the generations in various forms.

We have become so good at murdering!

We are murderers of the reputations of those in our circle of living in places like work, and dare I say, the church. Our own family members are most at risk of this violent crime.

We have become so proficient in character assassinations that we are even fooled by the schemes used to carry them out.
We so often do not recognize the sinister plans used to deliver the hurt and pain by the one perpetrating the effort (Satan himself) because time and again it is an inside job.

Position the importance of how you treat others within your circle of living using the following standard for behavior in the words of Jesus, and see how your world measures up:

"You have heard that it was said to the people long ago, 'You shall not murder, and anyone who murders will be subject to judgment.' But I tell you that anyone who is angry with a brother or sister will be subject to judgment. Again, anyone who says to a brother or sister, 'Raca,' is answerable to the court. And anyone who says, 'You fool!' will be in danger of the fire of hell. Therefore, if you are offering your gift at the altar and there remember that your brother or sister has something against you, leave your gift there in front of the altar. First go and be reconciled to them; then come and offer your gift" (Matthew 5:21-23).

Some of you are immediately saying, "Come on, isn't this a little radical? Aren't you taking this just a bit too far in your assessing a little family harshness and bad words to that of a comparison of murder?"

First of all, these aren't my words. And secondly, Jesus knows where anger can lead, and he is clearly wanting to stop the flow of anger before it can no longer be stopped.

The word "Raca" is an Aramaic term of, *contempt*. Contempt within the family is a very real emotion and challenge… and Jesus is giving us full warning here to dial it back, get a handle on what is happening, and honestly review the circumstances through his love. We cannot maintain meaningful long-term relationships, both in and out of our family, without managing our emotions. And we must manage these emotions in the Spirit of Christ's example to forgive; taking care of each event as they happen before moving on in our daily lives.

The opposite of living in the Spirit of Christ is the spirit of Cain, and we see the outcome of that lifestyle all over our communities, our nation and the world.

Consider this Scripture concerning this topic of bitterness and harshness leading to damaging attitudes and actions, even among those we should be closest to:

"For this is the message you heard from the beginning: We should love one another. Do not be like Cain, who belonged to the evil one and murdered his brother. And why did he murder him? Because his own actions were evil and his brother's were righteous. Anyone who hates a brother or sister is a murderer, and you know that no murderer has eternal life residing in him. This is how we know what love is: Jesus Christ laid down his life for us. And we ought to lay down our lives for our brothers and sisters" (I John 3:11, 12, 13-16).

There is that personal mission statement of Jesus again. Do you see it?

"… We ought to lay down our lives for our brothers and sisters."

Now, in many circles, the use of the words "brothers and sisters" are directed at fellow believers. But I believe they were also and originally meant for those that belong to us in our immediate family—to be taken literally.

I understand that this little conversation may seem a harsh description quite possibly by most of you reading this. However, the message of Jesus in Scripture is clear, in its teaching that we either maintain a Spirit of love and forgiveness in the legacy of Jesus, or the opposite will be true resulting in harshness, division, and even worse, in the spirit of Cain.

We must make a choice for our family and remain committed to putting away arguments and feelings of contempt as soon as they arise within our family, so we may maintain a home of purity in love as our foundation of family strength.

Live in Integrity

A Scripture passage that has always impacted my life, all of my life, is the following passage I am about to share with you.

It says to me that as Jesus stood in the midst of all the hate and accusation evil could muster, with no one present to speak on his behalf—no friends, no family—the following story was playing out:

"Then Pilate entered the Praetorium again, called Jesus, and said to Him, 'Are You the King of the Jews?'

Jesus answered him, 'Are you speaking for yourself about this, or did others tell you this concerning Me?'

Pilate answered, 'Am I a Jew? Your own nation and the chief priests have delivered You to me. What have You done?'

Jesus answered, 'My kingdom is not of this world. If My kingdom were of this world, My servants would fight, so that I should not be delivered to the Jews; but now My kingdom is not from here.'

Pilate therefore said to Him, 'Are You a king then?'

Jesus answered, 'You say *rightly* that I am a king. For this cause I was born, and for this cause I have come into the world, that I should bear witness to the truth. Everyone who is of the truth hears My voice.'

Pilate said to Him, 'What is truth?' And when he had said this, he went out again to the Jews, and said to them, '*I find no fault in Him at all*.'"

We must live a life such that when no words are offered in support of us, there is no true evidence of fault that can be found against us. We must live so that when there is no evidence to be offered against is, only the inaccurate words of hearsay of someone trying to do us harm, that those hearing these lying words simply say of us, "I cannot believe that to be true!"

Creating a reputation for life begins in the home in which we grow up and reside.

If those who know you best—having seen you live out your life each day as witnesses to whom you really and truly are—can support you in their belief in your personal integrity, even during the most difficult of moments, then your life, and the lives you impact, will consist of far more positive outcomes than failures.

In our vernacular we call it, "giving one the benefit of the doubt." It is the ability to believe in someone simply because they have lived in a manner that has made it possible to believe in them.

Does this speak to a person's perfection? No. It speaks to their motivations of heart. It speaks to them has having the heart of Jesus. Remember the description of David used by God himself when he was giving explanation as to why he chose David to be king and receive his blessing?

"After removing Saul, he made David their king. God testified concerning him: 'I have found David son of Jesse, *a man after my own heart*; he will do everything I want him to do'" (Acts 13:22).

Don't you think God knew the failures and sins that were coming in the life of David? That God knew the horrible decisions and actions that were going to emerge out of David's life?

But God also knew that, in the end, he would plead for forgiveness out of a genuine heart of repentance—eventually doing *everything God wanted him to do.*

2 Samuel Chapter 11 tells the entire story. God knew that after David's diabolical sin that ushered in the events of David stealing the wife (Bathsheba) of a good man (Uriah), fathering an illegitimate son, intentionally setting up the death of Uriah, and endeavoring to cover it all up in lies and deceit that led to the most chilling words of sentence ever spoken by a prophet (Nathan) of God to a mere mortal of a man stating, "… thou are the man!" (verse 7 of 2 Samuel Chapter 12) — God knew he would eventually hear these mournful words that would come from the very depths of David's heart, because God knew his heart:

"Have mercy on me, O God, according to your unfailing love; according to your great compassion blot out my transgressions. Wash away all my iniquity and cleanse me from my sin. Create in me a pure heart, O God, and renew a steadfast spirit within me. Do not cast me from your presence or take your Holy Spirit from me. Restore to me the joy of your salvation and grant me a willing spirit, to sustain me" (Psalm 51:1 and 2, 11 and 12).

When a person who lives in an effort to please God makes a grievous mistake—or even commits a wrongful sin—we can know that a person of integrity will respond in a heart of deep repentance and regret. And even greater, we know they will produce the effort to make the blunder right.

Why? Because they are a person after God's own heart, and they will eventually do what he wants them to do.

It is up to us, in the home, to give that person the opportunity to do just that; make a wrong right, allowing love and patience to rule the outcome, bringing a Godly conclusion into the imperfections of our lives and home. These teaching moments must come if we are to grow and allow others to grow into the kind of individuals God can use to better our world.

This is the example of Jesus to his family we must never forget.

Creating a family atmosphere of living within the forgiving spirit of granting the "benefit of the doubt" allows us to build toward living a life of integrity that reflects the words said about Jesus by even a man like Pilate to those bringing dire accusation against him, "I find no fault in Him at all."

Pilate was basically saying, "I simply can't believe that what you are saying he did is something he would do."

If we are creating a family environment that allows for finger pointing and accusation, instead of that of belief in one another and mutual support, we are setting the members of our family up for failure.

We must learn to live in a manner of integrity. *And integrity is only learned from our forgiven failures.*

We must establish a home where those who know us best have the opportunity to see us grow into our best.

And in achieving our best, a lot of forgiveness and renewal had to have taken place there. If this becomes the legacy of our home, we have already become successful in living as God intends for us to live—as a reflection of his perfection.

Chapter Thirteen

The Joy of Sacrifice

"In this world it is not what we take up,
but what we give up that makes us rich."
Henry Ward Beecher

13

A family begins to take great steps of achievement when we arrive at a place where we can pause to realize how much we do for each other without thinking of or weighing the sacrifice behind it.

The process, in a young family, begins in the little things, (not taking the last of something on the plate because you sense someone else is still hungry), and leads to some massive things, (a sibling donates a kidney, so his brother or sister could have a better quality of life—or more seriously yet—live.)

Let me deviate from my pattern of total reliance upon Scripture story telling about the family, for a moment of personal story telling about my own. I hope you don't mind.

I have two favorite pictures of my mother. One is of her in a hospital bed on an early October day just after I was born. The second is of me as a one-and-a-half-year-old little boy praying at my mother's knee. Sounds simple enough, yet it wasn't a simple journey at all.

My mother was learning that, for her at least, giving birth to a child was an extremely dangerous event. She had already miscarried once prior to my arrival on the scene. Both she and her doctor were on guard as to the possible complications that might be coming as the time grew nearer to my grand arrival.

When my mother went into labor for my birth, she was about to truly walk through the valley of the shadow of death to obtain an outcome originally designed to be the pure joy of giving birth to a new little life.
But the complications began to enter the equation, and as the labor grew more and more intense, so did the complications.

My mother would endure over forty hours of intense labor in the 1950's, (a time so very much different than that of today in terms of medical ability, procedure and understanding), to the point of nearly having to make some very difficult decisions as to whether to save herself or—me.

The plans and desires my mother had for her little baby far outweighed the immense challenges of giving birth. She had a vision for that little baby to which she devoted herself in preparation. She dedicated my life to the Lord before I was born as a major step toward the preparation of the completion of my days as the Lord saw fit. She took care of herself knowing full well the challenges that lay ahead. She stayed close to her own mother and doctor knowing the support and guidance that would be needed through teamwork in order to see the dream of a baby become real.

Then came the ordeal itself.

I believe there was an underlying battle afoot as to whether I was to be allowed to join the human race. It seems the cards were stacked against us. My mother's doctor, (eerily named, Dr. Graves), and his anesthesiologist, (I am not making this up—a young intern from the University of Michigan named, Dr. Jack Kevorkian. Yes, "Doctor Death," was on our team that October day) were the team overseeing my birth that day. And for those of you who are unaware of who Dr. Kevorkian was, he was known for his high-profile antics in support of voluntary euthanasia.

The efforts of the hospital staff and, most importantly—the Lord, allowed my mom to emerge finally in good health and for me to enter this world.

So why did I take the time to share with you this tiny nugget of my personal history? Simply because of a Scripture passage that set the tone for me in study for this writing as to why Jesus determined, with the Father and Holy Spirit, that he would come to this place and undergo all he had to brave, to deliver to us—if you will—life.

Here is that passage:

"Therefore we also, since we are surrounded by so great a cloud of witnesses, let us lay aside every weight, and the sin which so easily ensnares *us,* and let us run with endurance the race that is set before us, looking unto Jesus, the author and finisher of *our* faith, <u>who for the joy that was set before Him endured the cross</u>, despising the shame, and has sat down at the right hand of the throne of God" (Hebrews 12:1-2 NKJV)

What an amazing glimpse into the "why" of Jesus choosing to go through all he did in order to bring to us the priceless gift of life, joy, and fulfillment, into our personal lives and into our homes.

There it is for us to see ... "who for the joy that was set before Him endured the cross."

Isn't it so very similar to what a soon to be mommy faces when bringing a new little life into the world? The physical and mental stresses—and many times the accompanying dangers—are exceedingly real and powerful. Yet, when her baby comes, oh the instantaneous and exuberant joy! There is nothing so great as holding that sweet little newborn. It is in that loving first moment of bonding that the memory of what had just been endured has all but faded away for a new mommy.

How amazing it is!

Jesus never lost sight of his great goal for all generations. He set aside all, including his rights as God (Philippians 2:6, 7), to make everything that is "good" available to us through God the Father. Remember James 1:17?

"Whatever is good and perfect comes to us from God. He is the One Who made all light."

Remember, the cross is the final effective sacrifice for the battles of our lives—all our sins, and the vast number of ills that sin brought with it. And Jesus had to be made like us,

"... fully human in every way, in order that he might become a merciful and faithful high priest in service to God, and that he might make atonement for the sins of the people" (Hebrews 2:17).

He entered our world as a member of a family. This was his way of becoming and understanding what it is to be fully human—having to deal with the vast spectrum of emotions, both positive and negative, that come within that close-knit circle.

The target of evil is all the Father holds dear—his Son, his creation, and that most important of all within his creation, the family. The family has been the target of evil since the very beginning when Satan entered the scene in an effort to destroy Eve, the first mother of creation, and Adam, the first father.

God set out to rescue all his children through the greatest of all sacrifices, the death of his only Son on a cross (John 3:16).

In the deepest recesses of our being, we know this to be truth, and is why we would sacrifice anything—even our very lives—for our own children. This is one of the greatest of all proofs that we are made in His image (Genesis 1:27).
You may be having a hard time remembering the vision you originally had for your family due to some serious heavy struggle you are facing as you read this. Or you are simply in the middle of the struggle of everyday living and the daily rat race your lifestyle has become mired in. But I would challenge you to remember why you determined to have a family in the first place. Remember your original goals and dreams. And know too, that the prize is awaiting you, if you endure and defeat these difficulties between you and your joy in the strength and wisdom and touch of Jesus Christ.

Consider the words of Jesus in Scripture:

"Then he said to them all: "Whoever wants to be my disciple must deny themselves and take **up** their **cross** daily and follow me" (Luke 9:23).

When you deny yourself in loving sacrifice for your family, know the Lord is with you as you follow his example.

Endure your cross in reliance upon the guidance of the Father in prayer asking for wisdom, strength and direction; knowing your faithfulness—in the authority and leadership of Jesus—will bring you through your personal and family journey with the prize of joy. And know this too, that in the journey, he is making you and your family all he planned your household to be.

"Know therefore that the LORD your God is God; he is the faithful God, keeping his covenant of love to a thousand generations of those who love him and keep his commandments" (Deuteronomy 7:9).

He is faithful.

He is faithful to the generations.

He *will be* faithful to you!

CONCLUSION

Remember, even Christ's own family had major issues to overcome. Your family is not unique in this regard. But overcome them they did, and yours can too when you focus on Jesus and his love and legacy for your home. It is all about how his love for his family—the way he lived with and through them—impacts the way you live with and through your family, allowing *his* love to permeate your home.

In that thought, I leave you with this. When you allow the Spirit of Christ into your family, He will indeed change your entire household and your future. It was no accident that in Scripture, when a life was changed through belief in Christ, whole families were "saved" as a result of a single life changed. Beginning with your life, this can happen in your family too! Scripture shares these examples, so we know this to be true:

"Then the father realized that this was the exact time at which Jesus had said to him, 'Your son will live.' So he and his whole household believed" (John 4:53).

"He then brought them out and asked, 'Sirs, what must I do to be saved?'

They replied, 'Believe in the Lord Jesus Christ, and you will be saved—you and your household.'

The jailer brought them into his house and set a meal before them; he was filled with joy because he had come to believe in God—he and his whole household" (Acts 16:30, 31 and 34).

Believe in the Lord Jesus Christ, and you will be saved—you and your household.

Just as Jesus did for his family, he will do the same for yours.

ABOUT THE AUTHOR

Jerry Drummonds

As founder, Chairman, and CEO of Benchmark Living, Benchmark Verde, and Verde Energy, Gerald Vaughn "Jerry" Drummonds, spent much of his life with a focus in ministry having received his theological training and Ordination through Indiana Wesleyan University, Houghton College in Houghton, New York, and the Wesleyan Church.

The last decade plus, Jerry has been involved in developing key conclusionary approaches in the world of green energy design. Drummonds began this trek with other key thinkers and designers that eventually led to the founding of Verde Energy to bring a solution to the worldwide search for mainstream and back-up alternative fuel and power generation he believes God already made for the world.

Drummonds has over 35 years of business, publishing, creative, syndication, and product positioning in his past, producing or serving as the creator of or executive producer of radio programming aired on *ABC Radio, Westwood One, CBN Radio, Mutual* and *Armed Forces Radio*, along with hundreds of independently cleared stations around the world. He also produced the first ever Bible on tape through Zondervan.

The need to minister and witness directly to others as they face life's greatest choices, challenges, victories, and trials, through the life-changing message of the **Lord Jesus,** is the core to fulfillment in Jerry's life. This is where true personal spiritual growth comes for Jerry, and for all of us for that matter, as we share our faith with others using the giftings God has uniquely granted each of us.

The Family of Jesus

Timeless Lessons for Modern Families

From Benchmark Living

Made in the USA
Columbia, SC
13 August 2024